# Artificial intelligence:

# A Comprehensive Guide to Artificial Intelligence

# By

# Maula Lumena

# CONTENTS

## INTRODUCTION

"The science and engineering of making intelligent machines, especially intelligent computer programs". **-John McCarthy-**

**John McCarthy (1927-2011)** was an American computer scientist and cognitive scientist who is widely considered one of the founders of the field of artificial intelligence (AI). He is particularly known for his work on formalizing the notion of "artificial intelligence" and for developing the programming language Lisp.

**McCarthy** was born in Boston, Massachusetts, and earned his Ph.D. in mathematics from Princeton University in 1951. He taught at several universities throughout his career, including Stanford University, where he founded the Stanford AI Laboratory.

In addition to Lisp, McCarthy made important contributions to the development of several other programming languages, including Algol and Fortran. He also played a key role in the development of time-sharing systems, which allowed multiple users to access a computer simultaneously.

Throughout his career, McCarthy was a strong advocate for the use of computers to aid in human decision-making and problem-solving. He received numerous awards and honors for his work, including the Turing Award in 1971, the Kyoto Prize in 1988, and the National Medal of Science in 1991.

A computer, robot, or device may be made to think like a clever person by using artificial intelligence. Artificial Intelligence, or AI, investigates the ways in which the human brain works when it comes to solving issues. Finally, the results of this research are intelligent computer systems.

We may say that Artificial Intelligence is the capacity of a computer or robot to execute activities normally associated with intelligent individuals, or we can argue that it is a collection of algorithms that can create outcomes without being explicitly directed to do so. Artificial intelligence (AI) refers to the concept of intelligence displayed by computers.

| Definition |
|---|
| • A human-created intelligent being. |
| • Intelligently able to carry out things without being specifically told to do so. |
| • Ability to reason and behave in a compassionate manner. |

John McCarthy is widely considered one of the founders of the field of artificial intelligence (AI), and he was a strong advocate for the use of computers to aid in human decision-making and problem-solving.

**McCarthy** is credited with coining the term "artificial intelligence" in 1955, and he worked to formalize the notion of AI and develop techniques for creating intelligent machines. He saw AI as a way to automate tasks that are difficult or impossible for humans to perform, and he believed that intelligent machines could help solve complex problems in fields such as medicine, economics, and engineering.

However, McCarthy also recognized the potential dangers of AI and the need to ensure that intelligent machines would be designed and used in ethical and responsible ways. He was a vocal critic of "strong" AI, which he defined as the idea that machines could become conscious and surpass human intelligence. Instead, he advocated for "weak" AI, which refers to machines that are designed to perform specific tasks but do not have general intelligence or consciousness.

Overall, **McCarthy's** contributions to the field of artificial intelligence laid the groundwork for the development of modern AI technologies, and his insights on the risks and benefits of AI continue to influence research and development in the field today.

## HISTORY & FOUNDATIONS OF ARTIFICIAL INTELLIGENCE

The history of artificial intelligence (AI) can be traced back to ancient times, with references to automata and mechanical devices that could perform tasks that would otherwise require human labor. However, the modern field of AI began to take shape in the mid-20th century, when researchers began to develop computational techniques for creating intelligent machines.

One of the key early figures in AI was John McCarthy, who co-founded the field in 1956 at the Dartmouth Conference. At the conference, McCarthy and other researchers proposed a research program to develop intelligent machines that could reason, learn, and communicate like humans. This program laid the foundation for modern AI research and development.

In the decades that followed, AI researchers made significant progress in developing techniques such as expert systems, natural language processing, and machine learning. These technologies have been applied to a wide range of fields, including medicine, finance, and robotics.

However, the field of AI has also faced significant challenges and setbacks over the years, including funding cuts, criticisms of the field's hype, and concerns about the ethical implications of AI. These challenges have led to ongoing debates about the future of AI and how it should be developed and used.

Today, AI is a rapidly evolving field that continues to push the boundaries of what machines can do. The foundations of AI are built on a deep understanding of computer science, mathematics, and cognitive science, and the field is characterized by a diverse range of techniques and applications.

- **1943:** Warren McCulloch and Walter Pits performed the first work that would later become known as artificial intelligence (AI) in 1943. Within the framework of their paradigm, they advocated the deployment of artificial neurons.

- **1949:** The strength of neuronal connections may be altered by the use of an updating rule that was introduced by Donald Hebb. Learning using the Hebbian approach has now been given its own name.

- **1950:** Alan Turing, a British mathematician, is credited with making history in the year 1950 when he presented the concept of machine learning to the rest of the world. A test was offered in Alan Turing's book "Computing Machinery and Intelligence," which was released in 1950. It is possible to establish whether or not a computer can display intelligent behaviour that is equivalent to human intellect by using a test known as the Turing test.

o **1955:** Allen Newell and Herbert A. Simon are credited with the development of the "first artificial intelligence programme," which was given the name "Logic Theorist." Using this programme, which has already proved 38 of these 52 mathematical theorems, more sophisticated and original proofs were discovered for some of these mathematical theorems.

o **1956:** At the Dartmouth Conference, an American computer scientist named John McCarthy is credited with having first using the phrase "artificial intelligence." Because of this, artificial intelligence was finally acknowledged as a legitimate academic field for the very first time.

o **1966:** Algorithms for solving mathematical problems were a top priority for the researchers. Joseph Weizenbaum built the first chatbot, ELIZA, in 1966 and released it as a freeware programme.

o **1972:** It was the first intelligent humanoid robot ever built in Japan, and its name was WABOT-1.

o **1980:** "Expert System," the revived reaction of artificial intelligence That a direct consequence of this, computers have been programmed to make choices in the same manner as a knowledgeable human would.

- o **1997:** In 1997, IBM Deep Blue became the first computer to be victorious against a world chess champion when it triumphed over Gary Kasparov.

- o **2002:** The first artificial intelligence (AI) home appliance was the vacuum cleaner known as Roomba.

- o **2006:** The year 2006 marked the beginning of the commercial use of artificial intelligence (AI). Artificial intelligence is also being used by social media platforms like Facebook and Twitter, as well as streaming video services like Netflix.

- o **2011:** In 2011, IBM's Watson was able to interpret challenging questions and riddles, which led to the computer's victory on the game show Jeopardy! Watson has shown that it could understand normal language and quickly provide answers to challenging questions. o **2012:** "Google Now" is a new feature that was released by Google for its Android app. This function was able to predict what the user would want to do next based on their previous search history.

- o **2014:** In 2014, the "Turing test" competition was won by a chatbot that went by the name Eugene Goostman.

- o **2018:** The "Project Debater" software developed by IBM faced up against two very skilled debaters on a broad variety of topics, and it performed exceptionally well.

This amount of development in AI is quite astounding. The notion of deep learning, big data, and data science are currently sweeping the world. Artificial intelligence (AI) is now being used by major corporations like Google, Facebook, IBM, and Amazon to develop cutting-edge products.

## CHAPTER I: FOUNDATION OF ARTIFICIAL INTELLIGENCE

As a result of the Total Turing test, Stuart J. Russell and Peter Norvig divided AI into five separate study areas:

| |
|---|
| ➢ Machine Learning |
| ➢ Expert Systems |
| ➢ Computer Vision |
| ➢ Natural Language Processing |
| ➢ Robotics |

## Machine Learning

Machine learning is the field that examines how to educate computers so that they may learn on their own (ML). Computers can learn and comprehend patterns in pictures, audio, and other structured data using multidimensional arrays. The foundation for artificial intelligence may be found in this particular subject of study. In the field of machine learning, there are four distinct types of learning:

- **Supervised learning**: Using a new input array, it is possible to make predictions about both a labelled output variable such as sales, etc., and an array of characteristics such as week of the year, price, etc.

- **Unsupervised learning**: Perform an analysis on a variety of characteristics, such as demographic information, ZIP code, etc., and present any previously hidden correlations or anomalies.

- **Semi-supervised**: It is possible to make an educated guess as to the best possible estimations for the missing label variables by making use of a number of attributes and a constrained quantity of the labelled output variable.

- **Reinforcement learning**: An artificial agent may be trained to maximise its utility based on a user-defined utility function given a certain purpose.

| Expert Systems |
|:---:|

This kind of artificial intelligence (AI) is known as an expert system (ES) because it uses preprogrammed information to provide recommendations or make decisions. Elaborate if-then logic may be summarised as the following: If we want the computer to perform anything, we tell it to do z. There are various reasons why we would favour an ES over ML, despite the fact that ML has gotten a lot of attention recently.

- Knowledge gained via trial and error may be tapped into by an expert system.

- Expert systems are more predictable and less likely to produce severe mistakes when confronted with inputs they have never seen before.

- Historically, expert systems have been quicker and simpler to construct, but ML has become considerably more accessible in recent years.

---

## Computer Vision

Computer vision is the process of automatically extracting features from photographs or videos and analysing and interpreting those features (CV). By turning still images and moving images into numerical arrays, computer vision (CV) allows machine learning (ML) systems to draw inferences, make predictions, and even generate new pictures depending on user-defined inputs.

CV's potential applications have been explored for decades, but only lately have three improvements made CV a reality on a large scale:

- The creation of algorithms that are more efficient than those already in use: Deep learning convolution neural networks have seen significant improvements made to both their memory footprint and their computation runtime, particularly with regard to CV applications.

- Enhanced capacity for processing: It is now possible to run memory-intensive CV algorithms on graphics processing units (GPUs), distributed architectures like as Spark, and computing resources in the cloud that are quite inexpensive.

- Access to photos that may be used for training purposes: In order to train computer vision algorithms, a significant number of photographs that are available to the general public have been made available on social media platforms, community forums, digital cameras, and mobile cameras.

| |
|---|
| **Computer vision** is a field of artificial intelligence (AI) and computer science that focuses on enabling machines to interpret and understand visual information from the world around them. It involves developing algorithms and techniques that allow computers to analyze, process, and interpret digital images and videos. |
| Computer vision is used in a wide range of applications, including object recognition, image and video search, face recognition, surveillance, and autonomous vehicles. Some examples of computer vision applications in everyday life include facial recognition for unlocking smartphones, object detection in self-driving cars, and image search in online shopping platforms. |

To enable machines to interpret visual information, computer vision researchers develop algorithms and techniques that enable computers to analyze digital images and videos. These algorithms typically involve techniques such as image processing, feature extraction, object detection, and deep learning.

In recent years, deep learning has emerged as a particularly promising technique for enabling computers to perform complex visual tasks. Deep learning involves training neural networks to recognize patterns in data, such as images, and make predictions based on that data. This approach has been used to develop highly accurate image recognition and object detection systems, among other applications.

Computer vision has a wide range of real-world applications across various industries. Here are a few examples:

1. **Self-driving cars**: Computer vision plays a crucial role in enabling autonomous vehicles to navigate roads and avoid obstacles. Using cameras and sensors, self-driving cars can recognize and interpret road signs, traffic lights, and other vehicles on the road, allowing them to make informed decisions and avoid collisions.

2.  **Retail**: Computer vision can be used to enhance the shopping experience for customers in retail stores. For example, smart shelves equipped with cameras and sensors can detect when a customer takes a product off the shelf and automatically update inventory records. Facial recognition technology can also be used to personalize the shopping experience and provide targeted recommendations.

3.  **Healthcare**: Computer vision is increasingly being used in the healthcare industry to analyze medical images such as X-rays and MRIs. By training neural networks to recognize patterns in medical images, doctors can quickly and accurately diagnose diseases and identify abnormalities.

4.  **Security**: Computer vision can be used to improve security and surveillance systems. For example, facial recognition technology can be used to identify individuals in crowds or track suspects in real-time. Object detection algorithms can also be used to detect and alert security personnel to potential threats such as unattended bags or suspicious behavior.

## Natural Language Processing

Natural Language Processing (NLP) is a branch of artificial intelligence (AI) that focuses on enabling machines to understand, interpret, and generate human language. It involves developing algorithms and techniques that allow computers to analyze and derive meaning from natural language data, such as text and speech.

NLP is used in a wide range of applications, including language translation, sentiment analysis, chatbots, speech recognition, and text summarization. Some examples of NLP applications in everyday life include virtual assistants like Siri and Alexa, automated language translation services, and text-to-speech software.

To enable machines to understand and process natural language, NLP researchers develop algorithms and techniques that enable computers to recognize patterns in language data. These algorithms typically involve techniques such as statistical modeling, machine learning, and deep learning.

One of the major challenges in NLP is dealing with the ambiguity and complexity of human language. For example, words can have multiple meanings depending on the context in which they are used, and sentences can have multiple interpretations. NLP researchers develop techniques to address these challenges, such as part-of-speech tagging, named entity recognition, and semantic analysis.

There are several different types of natural language processing **(NLP)** systems. With the use of natural language processing **(NLP)** algorithms, meaning and purpose of the author may be inferred automatically by breaking down phrases into their constituent words, letters, or a combination of all of these. Use cases for NLP include:

| |
|---|
| • Recognition of named entities and resolution of conferences |
| • Part-of-speech tagging |
| • Reading comprehension and question responding |
| • Machine translation |
| • Text summarization and subject modelling |
| • Spell-check and auto-fill |

Siri and Alexa are two digital assistants that put the capability of natural language processing (NLP) on display by using "wake words" such as "play music," "search the web," "create to-do lists," and "control popular smart-home gadgets." These virtual assistants will continue to develop over time with the assistance of data collected from their existing users, the development of new use cases, and integration with their present organisations.

## Robotics

**Robotics** is the study of designing, constructing, programming, and using robots to solve problems faced by humans in their environment. Given the wide variety of robots now in existence, it may be challenging to pin down the precise meaning of the term "robot."

New designs and application cases that seem to be lifted directly from a science fiction book have been made possible by the fast advancements in robotics research over the last decade. Manufacturers working in certain fields continue to push the boundaries of robots.

- Humanoid robot Boston Dynamics, a pioneer in the field, continues to advance its technology.

- DJI has made it simpler than ever for the ordinary individual to fly a drone thanks to its concentration on consumer-grade models.

- Amazon's logistics strategy relies heavily on Amazon Robotics, which saves the retail giant billions of dollars each year.

## QUESTIONS AND ANSWERS

Q: When did the field of artificial intelligence first emerge?
A: The field of artificial intelligence (AI) emerged in the 1950s, with the development of electronic computers and the realization that machines could be used to simulate human intelligence.

Q: Who are some of the pioneers of artificial intelligence?
A: Some of the pioneers of AI include John McCarthy, Marvin Minsky, Claude Shannon, and Allen Newell.

Q: What are some of the early milestones in AI research? A: Some of the early milestones in AI research include the development of the Logic Theorist program in 1956, the creation of the first AI programming language (LISP) in 1958, and the development of the perceptron algorithm for pattern recognition in 1957.

Q: What are some of the different approaches to artificial intelligence? A: There are several different approaches to AI, including rule-based systems, symbolic AI, connectionist AI, and evolutionary AI.

Q: What is the Turing test? A: The Turing test, proposed by British mathematician and computer scientist Alan Turing in 1950, is a test of a machine's ability to exhibit intelligent behavior that is indistinguishable from that of a human.

Q: What are some of the challenges facing AI research today? A: Some of the challenges facing AI research today include developing algorithms that can learn from small or incomplete datasets, ensuring that AI systems are transparent and explainable, and addressing concerns around bias and ethical issues.

Q: What are some of the applications of artificial intelligence? A: AI is used in a wide range of applications, including image and speech recognition, natural language processing, predictive analytics, autonomous systems, and robotics.

Q: What is the difference between narrow AI and general AI? A: Narrow AI refers to AI systems that are designed to perform a specific task or set of tasks, while general AI refers to AI systems that have the ability to perform any intellectual task that a human can. General AI is still largely a hypothetical concept.

## CHAPTER II: USES OF ARTIFICIAL INTELLIGENCE

By the day, Artificial Intelligence is becoming more and more useful and popular. The capacity of a system or a computer to think and learn through experience is known as artificial intelligence. The use of artificial intelligence (AI) in business has grown dramatically in recent years and has found its way into practically every industry.

### 1. AI Application in E-Commerce

**Personalized Shopping**

Recommendation engines built with artificial intelligence technologies may help you build stronger relationships with your consumers. These suggestions are based on the user's previous browsing habits, preferences, and personal interests. It's a great way to build stronger bonds with your clients and increase consumer loyalty to your company.

**AI-powered Assistants**

Chatbots and virtual shopping assistants may enhance the online buying experience for customers. In order to make the dialogue seem as real and intimate as possible, Natural Language Processing is employed. In addition, these assistants may interact with your consumers in real time.

Customer care on Amazon.com may soon be handled by chatbots, as you may have heard.

**Fraud Prevention**

Fraudulent credit card transactions and phoney customer reviews are two of the most common problems E-Commerce enterprises face. AI may assist lower the likelihood of credit card theft by analysing use trends. Consumers are increasingly relying on online reviews to help them make purchasing decisions. Detecting and dealing with fraudulent reviews may be made easier with the use of artificial intelligence (AI).

## 2. Applications Of Artificial Intelligence in Education

### Administrative Tasks Automated to Aid Educators

In an educational setting, artificial intelligence can assist with non-educational tasks such as facilitating and automating personalised messages to students, back-office tasks such as grading paperwork, organising and facilitating interactions with parents and guardians, routine issue feedback facilitation, managing enrollment, courses, and HR-related topics, and more.

### Creating Smart Content

With the use of artificial intelligence, it is possible to digitise educational materials such as video lectures, conferences, and textbook manuals. Students of all grades may benefit from a variety of interfaces, such as animations and personalised learning material.

By producing and presenting audio and video summaries, as well as lesson plans, AI helps to provide a rich learning experience.

## Voice Assistants

Students may use Voice Assistants to get additional resources and help even if their lecturers or teachers aren't there. It is possible to save money on printing expenses for short-term handbooks, as well as providing solutions to frequently asked topics.

## Personalized Learning

For the purpose of keeping a close check on student data and simply producing things like study habits, lesson plans, reminders, study aids, flash notes, and the frequency with which students should be revising their work, hyper-personalization techniques that are based on AI may be used.

## 3. Applications of Artificial Intelligence in Lifestyle

## Autonomous Vehicles

When it comes to driving in any environment and recognising objects, companies like Toyota, Audi, Volvo, and Tesla use machine learning to teach computers how to think and develop as naturally as people do. This helps them avoid getting into accidents.

**Spam Filters**

Emails that are identified as spam are routed automatically to the spam or trash folders of our email accounts. Here, we are only able to read the content that has been filtered. Gmail, one of the most widely used email services, has a filtering capability that is around 99.9 percent effective.

## Facial Recognition

Facial recognition technology is used by our favourite gadgets, such as smartphones, laptops, and desktop computers, to detect and identify users for the purpose of securing access. Facial recognition is a commonly utilised AI application outside of personal use, even in high-security settings in a variety of sectors.

## Recommendation System

Ecommerce, entertainment, social networking, video sharing platforms like YouTube, etc. all utilise the recommendation system to collect user data and deliver personalised suggestions to users in order to boost their involvement with these platforms. All sectors utilise this AI programme, and it's quite popular.

## 4. Applications of Artificial intelligence in Navigation

According to the findings of a research conducted at MIT, the usage of GPS technology may contribute to an improvement in user safety by supplying users with information that is both timely and accurate. The use of Convolution Neural Networks and Graph Neural Networks makes it possible to carry out automated identification of the number of lanes and kinds of roads that lie behind obstructions that are located along a roadway. Utilizing artificial intelligence may help improve operational efficiency, as well as assess and optimise road traffic and route optimization (AI).

## 5. Applications of Artificial Intelligence in Robotics

An artificial intelligence application is also employed in robotics. Robots powered by artificial intelligence (AI) employ real-time updates to detect obstructions in its path and pre-plan its route immediately. Uses include transporting supplies and equipment in healthcare facilities and industrial facilities, cleaning offices and huge equipment, and keeping track of inventories. **6. Applications of Artificial Intelligence in Social Media**

| *Instagram* |
| --- |

In order to select what posts you see on Instagram's Explore page, AI takes into consideration your likes and follows.

### Facebook

Artificial Intelligence (AI) and a programme called DeepText are also used. Facebook will be able to better grasp discussions going on thanks to this new technology. It may be used to automatically translate postings from many languages.

### Twitter

Twitter uses artificial intelligence (AI) to discover and remove fraud, misinformation, and offensive material. Users' engagement with tweets is used as a basis to propose other tweets that they may appreciate.

## 7. Applications of Artificial Intelligence in Marketing

- Marketers may use behavioural analysis, pattern recognition, and other AI techniques to provide highly targeted and customised advertisements. It also aids in the timely retargeting of audiences for improved outcomes and less sentiments of mistrust and frustration.

- Content marketing may benefit from AI's ability to mimic the brand's tone and style. For example, it may be used to track campaign performance and much more.

- Chatbots powered by AI, Natural Words Processing, Natural Language Generation, and Natural Language Understanding can evaluate the user's language and answer in the same manner as people do.

- Chatbots powered by AI, Natural Words Processing, Natural Language Generation, and Natural Language Understanding can evaluate the user's language and answer in the same manner as people do.

---

**QUESTIONS AND ANWERS**

---

Q: What are some examples of AI in everyday life? A: Some examples of AI in everyday life include virtual assistants like Siri and Alexa, recommendation algorithms used by online retailers and streaming services, and image and speech recognition technology used in smartphones and cameras.

Q: How is AI used in healthcare? A: AI is used in healthcare for a variety of applications, including diagnostic imaging, drug discovery, and personalized medicine. For example, AI algorithms can analyze medical images to detect signs of disease, or analyze patient data to identify optimal treatments.

Q: How is AI used in finance? A: AI is used in finance for tasks such as fraud detection, portfolio management, and risk assessment. For example, AI algorithms can analyze financial transactions to identify patterns that may indicate fraud, or analyze market data to identify opportunities for investment.

Q: How is AI used in manufacturing? A: AI is used in manufacturing for tasks such as quality control, predictive maintenance, and supply chain management. For example, AI algorithms can analyze sensor data from production lines to detect defects, or analyze historical data to predict when equipment may require maintenance.

Q: How is AI used in transportation? A: AI is used in transportation for tasks such as autonomous vehicle navigation, traffic management, and predictive maintenance. For example, AI algorithms can analyze sensor data from vehicles to detect hazards or optimize routes, or analyze data from maintenance records to predict when vehicles may require repairs.

Q: How is AI used in education? A: AI is used in education for tasks such as personalized learning, automated grading, and student engagement. For example, AI algorithms can analyze student performance data to identify areas where individual students may require additional support or challenge, or provide interactive learning experiences using natural language processing technology.

Q: What are some of the ethical considerations around the use of AI? A: Ethical considerations around the use of AI include concerns around bias and fairness, privacy and security, and the impact of automation on employment and society as a whole. It is important to design AI systems that are transparent and accountable, and to ensure that the benefits of AI are distributed fairly.

## CHAPTER III: BENEFITS & LIMITATIONS OF ARTIFICIAL INTELLIGENCE

A computer program's intelligence is referred to be artificial. Everything that includes a software accomplishing something that we would typically assume relies on the intellect of a human being might be deemed artificial intelligence.

Artificial intelligence applications may change every industry, and the benefits are huge. Here are a few examples:

### 1) Reduction in Human Error:

Because people make errors, the term "human error" was coined. When computers are correctly designed, however, they do not commit these kinds of blunders. Artificial intelligence (AI) relies on algorithms to make judgments based on data that has already been collected. Because of this, it is possible to achieve more precision while also reducing mistakes.

**Example:** Most human error has been removed from Weather Forecasting using AI.

### 2) Takes risks instead of Humans:

This is one of the most significant benefits of AI. We can get around many of the dangerous constraints that people have by creating an AI robot that can take on the dangerous tasks on our behalf. No matter what the situation calls for, whether it's travelling to Mars, disarming a bomb, penetrating the ocean's depths, or mining for coal and oil, this technology may be put to good use.

**Example:** Have you heard about the disaster at Ukraine's Chernobyl nuclear power plant? Because humans were instantly killed when they got too near to the centre of the disaster, there were no AI-powered robots available to assist us reduce the radiation's impact. They ultimately used helicopters to drop sand and boron from a short distance away.

There are instances in which human assistance may be dangerous, and AI robots can help.

### 3) Available 24x7:

Including breaks, an average person will labour between four and six hours a day. Humans are designed to take breaks to replenish and prepare for the next day's work, and they even have weekly off to keep work and personal lives separate. It's possible to have robots operate around the clock with no pauses or boredom thanks to artificial intelligence (AI).

**Example:** Artificial Intelligence (AI) may help educational institutions and helpline centres manage a wide range of enquiries and concerns more efficiently.

### 4) Assistance with Boring Jobs:

Sending thank you notes, checking papers for faults, and many other tasks will be part of our daily routine. It is possible to use artificial intelligence to effectively automate and even eliminate "boring" work for people, allowing them to free themselves up to be more creative.

**Example:** Verifying paperwork is a common sight at banks, and it is one that the bank's owner has to deal with again and time again. By using AI Cognitive Automation, the owner will be able to expedite the verification process, which will benefit both consumers and the owner.

### 5) Digital Assistance:

Digital assistants are being used by some of the world's most technologically proficient enterprises to reduce their reliance on human staff. Many websites also utilise digital assistants to fulfil the needs of their visitors. They'll be able to help us find what we need. When it comes to certain chatbots, it's difficult to tell if we're conversing with an actual person or an artificial intelligence.

**Example:** We are all aware that businesses have a customer service department whose job it is to answer customers' questions and concerns. AI may be used to create a voice or chatbot that can answer consumers' questions. For example, a number of businesses have already used them on their websites and mobile apps.

### 6) Faster Decisions:

We can speed up machine decision-making and action by combining AI with other technologies. AI-powered machines, on the other hand, focus only on what they've been trained to do and offer the findings in a more efficient manner when making a choice.

**Example:** We've all used Windows to play chess. This game's AI is so advanced that it's practically impossible for a human to defeat the CPU on hard mode. According to the algorithms that drive it, it will take the best possible step in the shortest amount of time.

**8) New Inventions:**

Humans will soon have the ability to tackle most of the world's most difficult issues thanks to the capacity of artificial intelligence (AI).

**Example:** Recently, physicians have been able to use AI-based technology to predict breast cancer in women at an earlier stage.

As with everything, there is a shadow side. There are however some **drawbacks** to artificial intelligence. Here are a few examples:

**1) High Costs of Creation:**

In order to keep up with the ever-changing needs of AI, hardware and software must also be kept up to date. There is a lot of money involved in repairing and maintaining machines. It needs a lot of money to build since they are very complicated machinery.

## 2) Making Humans Lazy:

Artificial intelligence (AI) is making people lazy by automating the bulk of their tasks. Future generations may face a dilemma if humans get hooked to these new technology.

## 3) Unemployment:

AI is replacing the bulk of the repetitious and other duties with robots, and this will have a huge impact on employment standards. AI robots that can do comparable tasks faster and more efficiently are being sought by every company to take the place of humans with the bare minimum of qualifications.

## 4) No Emotions:

There is no question that robots are more efficient than humans, but they cannot replace the human connection that is the core of the team. When it comes to managing a team, a humanto-human relationship is crucial, and machines don't have this ability.

## 5) Lacking Out of Box Thinking:

If a machine is not built or configured to accomplish a certain job, it is likely to malfunction or provide erroneous results.

## QUESTIONS AND ANSWERS

Q: What are some of the benefits of artificial intelligence?
A: Some of the benefits of artificial intelligence include increased efficiency and productivity, improved decision-making, and enhanced accuracy and precision. AI can also enable new applications and solutions that were not possible before.

Q: How can AI be used to improve healthcare outcomes? A: AI can be used in healthcare to improve outcomes by enabling faster and more accurate diagnoses, identifying optimal treatments for individual patients, and predicting and preventing potential health problems before they occur.

Q: What are some of the limitations of artificial intelligence? A: Some of the limitations of artificial intelligence include the potential for bias and errors in decision-making, the lack of creativity and intuition, and the difficulty of replicating human-like cognition and consciousness.

Q: How can bias be addressed in AI systems? A: Bias can be addressed in AI systems by ensuring that datasets used to train AI algorithms are diverse and representative, and by designing algorithms that are transparent and explainable.

Regular audits and evaluations of AI systems can also help to identify and mitigate bias.

Q: What are some ethical concerns surrounding the use of AI? A: Ethical concerns surrounding the use of AI include the potential for misuse or abuse, the impact on employment and inequality, and the responsibility for decisions made by AI systems. It is important to ensure that AI is used in ways that are transparent, fair, and accountable.

Q: How can AI be used to improve environmental sustainability? A: AI can be used to improve environmental sustainability by enabling more efficient resource use and management, identifying and predicting environmental risks, and developing new solutions for renewable energy and waste reduction.

Q: How can AI be used in education? A: AI can be used in education to provide personalized learning experiences, automate grading and feedback, and support student engagement and motivation. AI can also be used to provide more efficient and effective training for educators.

Q: What are some of the challenges facing the widespread adoption of AI? A: Some of the challenges facing the widespread adoption of AI include the need for large amounts of high-quality data, the complexity and cost of developing AI systems, and concerns around privacy, security, and ethical issues.

## CHAPTER IV: CHALLENGES & RISKS IN ARTIFICIAL INTELLIGENCE

### Challenges in AI:

### 1. Computing Power

Because of how much power they use, the vast majority of software developers avoid using these resource-intensive algorithms. Machine Learning and Deep Learning are important stepping stones on the path to artificial intelligence. These two types of learning need everincreasing numbers of processors and graphics processing units (GPUs). These frameworks have applications in a wide variety of fields, including the monitoring of asteroids and the creation of healthcare systems.

### 2. Trust Deficit

One of the biggest concerns about AI is the uncertainty of how deep learning algorithms forecast their results. It is difficult to comprehend how a single set of inputs may be used to solve a variety of distinct issues.

### 3. Limited Knowledge

Artificial Intelligence can be a superior option to conventional systems in many cases, although this is not always the case. The underlying issue is the lack of understanding about AI. There are just a small number of individuals who are aware of AI's potential, including technology enthusiasts, college students, and researchers.

## 4. Human-level

AI researchers have been on edge for years as a result of this problem, which is one of the most significant in the field. In all of these cases, human beings can outperform these corporations, even if they claim to be 90% accurate. Let our model, for example, determine if the picture depicts a dog or a cat. Humans have a remarkable level of accuracy in predicting the right result approximately 100% of the time.

## 5. Data Privacy and Security

The performance of deep learning and machine learning models is mostly determined by the amount of data and resources that are readily available for training these models. Because this information was compiled by millions of individuals from different parts of the globe, there is a chance that it may be utilised in an inappropriate manner.

## 6. The Bias Problem

The amount of information that is used in the training of an artificial intelligence system has a major bearing on the quality of the AI system that is produced. As a consequence of this, the key to effectively building AI systems in the future is going to be on acquiring data of a high quality. However, there is a challenge associated with the data that is collected on a regular basis by enterprises.

## 7. Data Scarcity

It is becoming more common for nations like India to impose tough IT regulations in order to limit the flow of user data created by large businesses like Google, Facebook, and Apple. As a consequence, these businesses are now confronted with the dilemma of designing global apps utilising local data, which would introduce bias.

## Risks of Artificial Intelligence

Risks linked with artificial intelligence will continue to increase as its capabilities and prevalence grows. In this essay, I'll discuss five of the most prevalent concerns associated with artificial intelligence that are now in existence.

## 1. Lack of AI Implementation Traceability

We frequently begin with a list of systems and models that contain artificial intelligence when it comes to risk management. We can monitor, analyse, prioritise, and manage AI risks by using a risk universe.

## 2. Introducing Program Bias into Decision Making

Artificial intelligence's decision-making processes might be impacted by human bias. Depending on how the dataset was compiled, it may include biases or preconceptions. The system's decision-making may be affected by its biases.

### 3. Data Sourcing and Violation of Personal Privacy

The global datasphere will have 175 zettabytes of data by 2025, up from 33 zettabytes in 2018. Companies have access to massive amounts of organised and unstructured data. As this field develops tremendously, consumer and employee data exposure risks will grow and privacy will be harder to safeguard. Data breaches and leaks may damage a company's reputation and lead to legal action, since many governments prohibit the usage of personal data. The EU's 2016 General Data Protection Regulation (GDPR) influenced California's 2018 Consumer Privacy Act.

### 4. Black Box Algorithms and Lack of Transparency

Even the individuals who designed AI systems may not completely understand how they make predictions. Due of a lack of transparency, some algorithms are called "black boxes," and lawmakers are looking at possible checks and balances. Companies risk being unable to justify why an AI-based creditworthiness projection is refused.

### 5. Unclear Legal Responsibility

This raises an issue of legal accountability in light of the possible dangers of artificial intelligence that have been considered so far. So who is legally accountable if an AI system is constructed with fuzzy algorithms and machine learning enables the decision-making to be refined itself? Is it the corporation, the programmer, or the system that's at fault? In 2018, a pedestrian was murdered by a self-driving automobile. This is not a theoretical concern. As a result, when the car's human backup driver got distracted, the AI system failed.

## QUESTIONS AND ANSWERS

Q: What are some of the ethical risks associated with the use of AI? A: Ethical risks associated with the use of AI include the potential for bias and discrimination, lack of transparency and accountability, and risks to privacy and security.

Q: What are some of the risks associated with the use of autonomous systems? A: Risks associated with the use of autonomous systems include the potential for accidents or errors, difficulty in assigning responsibility for actions taken by autonomous systems, and the potential for malicious use.

Q: How can bias be addressed in AI systems? A: Bias can be addressed in AI systems by ensuring that datasets used to train AI algorithms are diverse and representative, and by designing algorithms that are transparent and explainable. Regular audits and evaluations of AI systems can also help to identify and mitigate bias.

Q: What are some of the challenges associated with developing ethical AI? A: Challenges associated with developing ethical AI include the difficulty of defining ethical principles and values, the complexity of implementing ethical decision-making in AI systems, and the need to balance competing ethical concerns.

Q: How can cybersecurity risks associated with AI be addressed? A: Cybersecurity risks associated with AI can be addressed by implementing robust security measures, such as encryption, access controls, and regular audits and testing. AI systems should also be designed with security in mind, and security should be a key consideration throughout the development process.

Q: What are some of the challenges associated with the development of AI talent and skills? A: Challenges associated with the development of AI talent and skills include the high demand for skilled professionals, the rapid pace of technological change, and the need for interdisciplinary skills and knowledge.

Q: What are some of the challenges associated with regulating AI? A: Challenges associated with regulating AI include the difficulty of defining and enforcing standards for AI systems, the complexity of regulating rapidly evolving technology, and the need for international cooperation and coordination.

Q: What are some of the social and economic risks associated with AI? A: Social and economic risks associated with AI include the potential for job displacement, increased inequality, and the concentration of power and wealth in the hands of a few large technology companies. It is important to address these risks to ensure that the benefits of AI are distributed fairly.

# CHAPTER V: SEARCH ALGORITHM IN ARTIFICIAL INTELLIGENCE

In the field of Artificial Intelligence, search algorithms are one of the most essential.

**Problem-solving agents**:

In AI problem solving, search techniques are a common method. Algorithms and search tactics used by AI rational agents or problem solvers are commonly referred to as "algorithms." These are the problem-solving agents that use atomic representations. In this session, we'll cover a number of search techniques for solving issues.

Search Algorithm Terminologies:

- **Search:** In a predefined search region, searching is a strategy for finding a solution to a search problem in a stepwise approach. If you're having trouble finding anything, you should focus on these three things:

    **Search Space:** Search space is a collection of all possible solutions possessed by a system.

    **Start State:** This is where the hunt begins for agents.

    **Goal test:** Monitors the current state to see whether or not it has reached the target state, and returns if it has.

**Search tree:** Tree-like representations of a search problem are known as "search trees." We begin our research here, as the name says.

**Actions:** In order to help the agent, it gives a list of all available actions.

**Transition model:** With a transition diagram, you can demonstrate what each action does.

**Path Cost:** It's a function that assigns a monetary value to each different route.

**Solution:** It is a chain of occurrences that moves forward from the beginning to the conclusion of the story.

**Optimal Solution:** whether a solution is the most cost-effective of all the options that are accessible.

Properties of Search Algorithms:

Search algorithms have four basic qualities that may be used to compare their efficiency:

**Completeness:** If at least one solution exists for any random input, a search method is considered to be complete.

**Optimality:** The optimal solution for an algorithm is the one that is certain to be the best answer (the one with the lowest route cost) out of all the other potential options.

**Time Complexity:** The time complexity of an algorithm is a measurement of how much time it takes for the algorithm to complete its task.

**Space Complexity:** It's the greatest amount of storage space needed at any given stage in the search due to the problem's complexity.

Types of search algorithms

**Uninformed/Blind Search**: In an uninformed search, the target's position and proximity are unknown. It doesn't traverse the tree and identify leaf and goal nodes. The search tree is searched without any information about the search space, such as initial state operators and objective tests. It inspects each node till reaching the target node.

**It can be divided into five main types:**

- o Breadth-first search

- o Uniform cost search

- o Depth-first search

- o Iterative deepening depth-first search

- o Bidirectional Search

**Informed Search**: Search engines that are knowledgeable about a certain subject are more likely to provide relevant results. Information about the situation may be used to lead an educated search. A solution may be found more quickly with well-informed search tactics than with ill-informed ones. Heuristic search is another name for informed search.

A heuristic may provide a respectable solution in a reasonable period of time, but not the best. An intelligent search may uncover a solution to a difficult problem. Traveling salesman problem uses intelligent search methods.

1. Greedy Search

2. A* Search

| QUESTIONS AND ANSWERS |
| --- |

Q: What is a search algorithm in artificial intelligence? A: A search algorithm is a method used to find a solution or a path from an initial state to a goal state in a problem-solving task. It involves exploring a space of possible solutions to find the optimal solution.

Q: What are some common types of search algorithms used in AI? A: Some common types of search algorithms used in AI include breadth-first search, depth-first search, uniform-cost search, A* search, and iterative deepening search.

Q: What is breadth-first search? A: Breadth-first search is a search algorithm that explores all the neighboring nodes at the present depth level before moving on to the next level. It is used to find the shortest path between two nodes.

Q: What is depth-first search? A: Depth-first search is a search algorithm that explores as far as possible along each branch before backtracking. It is used to explore all possible solutions to a problem.

Q: What is uniform-cost search? A: Uniform-cost search is a search algorithm that finds the path between two nodes with the lowest cost. It takes into account the cost of each step taken along the way.

Q: What is A* search? A: A* search is a search algorithm that combines the advantages of both breadth-first search and uniform-cost search. It uses a heuristic function to guide the search towards the goal state while taking into account the cost of each step.

Q: What is iterative deepening search? A: Iterative deepening search is a search algorithm that combines the advantages of both depth-first search and breadth-first search. It performs a series of depth-limited searches, increasing the depth limit with each iteration until the goal state is reached.

Q: What are some considerations when choosing a search algorithm for a problem? A: Some considerations when choosing a search algorithm for a problem include the size of the problem space, the available resources, the nature of the problem, and the desired properties of the solution. Different algorithms may be more suitable for different types of problems.

## CHAPTER VI: ARTIFICIAL INTELLIGENCE IN CYBER SECURITY

Cyber security is one of the most challenging challenges we face, and AI is well-suited to help us address it. Machine learning and AI may be used to "keep up with the bad guys," automating threat detection and responding more quickly than conventional software-driven techniques to today's continually developing cyber-attacks and proliferation of gadgets.

At the same time, cyber security presents some unique challenges:

> ➤ A large attack area

➢ More than a few thousand devices per company
➢ Many different ways to get in
➢ There are serious shortages of qualified security personnel.
➢ Large amounts of data that are no longer only an issue on a human scale

These problems can be solved with a self-learning, AI-based cyber security posture management system. Technology is available to correctly train a self-learning system to continually and autonomously collect data from all of the company's IT systems. In order to conduct correlations of patterns across millions to billions of signals relevant to the corporate attack surface, this data is then evaluated and utilised to accomplish

This has resulted in unprecedented levels of intelligence being sent to human cyber security teams in a wide range of areas, such as:

- **IT Asset Inventory** – Accurately cataloguing all devices, users, and apps that have access to information systems. Additionally, inventory management relies heavily on categorization and assessment of business criticality.

- **Threat Exposure** – Hackers are no different from the rest of us in that they keep up with the latest fashions. It's possible to utilise artificial intelligence-based cyber security systems to stay on top of global and industry-specific risks, which may help you prioritise threats that might be used to attack your company as well as those that are most likely to be used against it.

- **Controls Effectiveness** – Understanding the effect of the different security tools and procedures you've implemented is critical to maintaining a strong security posture. AI can assist you identify the strengths and weaknesses of your information security programme.

- **Breach Risk Prediction** – AI-based solutions may predict how and where you'll be compromised, letting you to target resources and equipment to vulnerable points. AI analysis may be used to customise and optimise cyber security policies and processes.

- **Incident response** – An AI-powered system can prioritise and react to security alerts, swiftly respond to issues, and find underlying reasons to correct vulnerabilities and avoid future problems.

- **Explainability** – Using AI to complement human information security teams requires that advice and analyses be understandable. Stakeholders across the organisation, including end users, security operations and CISO, auditors, CIO and board of directors, need to be involved in this process in order to understand the impact of various information security programmes, and to report relevant information to all stakeholders.

---

## QUESTIONS AND ANSWERS

Q: How can artificial intelligence improve cybersecurity? A: Artificial intelligence can improve cybersecurity in various ways, such as identifying and mitigating threats faster, analyzing vast amounts of data, detecting anomalies, automating tasks, and improving accuracy.

Q: What are some applications of artificial intelligence in cybersecurity? A: Some applications of artificial intelligence in cybersecurity include threat detection and response, malware detection and analysis, network traffic analysis, user behavior analytics, vulnerability assessment, and fraud detection.

Q: What are some challenges of using artificial intelligence in cybersecurity? A: Some challenges of using artificial intelligence in cybersecurity include the lack of high-quality data, the need for skilled personnel to develop and maintain AI systems, the potential for AI systems to generate false positives or false negatives, and the risk of adversaries using AI for cyberattacks.

Q: How can machine learning be used for cybersecurity? A: Machine learning can be used for cybersecurity in various ways, such as identifying patterns and anomalies in data, detecting and classifying malware, predicting and preventing cyberattacks, and improving incident response.

Q: What is anomaly detection in cybersecurity? A: Anomaly detection is a technique used to identify patterns in data that deviate from normal behavior. It can be used in cybersecurity to detect potential threats or malicious activity.

Q: How can natural language processing be used in cybersecurity? A: Natural language processing can be used in cybersecurity to analyze text-based data, such as emails, social media messages, and chat logs. It can be used to detect phishing attempts, identify malicious content, and classify messages based on their level of threat.

Q: What is a security information and event management (SIEM) system? A: A security information and event management (SIEM) system is a tool that collects and analyzes security-related data from various sources, such as logs and network traffic. It can use machine learning and other AI techniques to detect and respond to security incidents.

Q: How can AI be used for threat hunting? A: AI can be used for threat hunting by analyzing large amounts of data and identifying potential threats that may have gone unnoticed. It can also be used to automate certain aspects of threat hunting, such as gathering data and correlating events.

## CHAPTER VII: NATURAL LANGUAGE PROCESSING IN ARTIFICIAL INTELLIGENCE

**An artificial intelligence area** called natural language processing (NLP) is concerned with helping computers comprehend how people write and communicate. The sheer volume of unstructured data makes this a challenging undertaking. People's 'tone of voice', or the way they speak and write, is distinctive to each person and continually altering to reflect the current zeitgeist.

Contextual understanding is likewise a problem, requiring semantic analysis before machine learning can grasp it. These subtleties are dealt with by natural language understanding (NLU) as a sub-branch of NLP, rather than just interpreting literal meanings. Computers can only communicate naturally with one another if NLP and NLU are used to assist them grasp human language.

The following are some examples of NLP in action in the real world:

- o Artificial intelligence (AI) systems such as Siri and Alexa.
- o Chatbots may use natural language generation to answer customers' questions.
- o Streamlining the hiring process by skimming through people's stated talents and experience on LinkedIn.

- o Grammarly, for example, uses NLP to assist detect mistakes and give recommendations for streamlining difficult text.
- o Models that learn from previous input to anticipate the next words in a text, such as auto-complete.

Computers learn from us when we use them often. Google Translate's Google Neural Machine Translation technology uses iterative learning (GNMT). GNMT improves linguistic fluency and accuracy. GNMT translates phrases, not just words. GNMT uses millions of translations to broaden its context. Instead of creating an interlingua, it compares languages. GNMT uses "zero-shot translate" instead of the lengthy process of translating from the source language into English before translating to the target language.

NLP is commonly utilised in healthcare, even though Google Translate isn't quite up to the task of translating medical instructions. Unstructured data from electronic health record systems is especially valuable in aggregating information from this tool. In addition to being unstructured, physicians' case notes may be inconsistent and utilise many distinct terms as a result of the difficulty of utilising often cumbersome systems. For example, NLP may be used to uncover previously undiscovered or incorrectly coded circumstances.

Depending on the study, natural language processing may be arranged using different machine learning algorithms. Simple things like use frequency or emotional connection might be difficult. Any application requires an algorithm. The Natural Language Toolkit (NLTK) uses Python libraries and programmes to analyse English natural language statistically and symbolically. Tokenization (word segmentation) and other NLP tasks like part-of-speech tagging and text classification datasets may benefit.

Sorting and coding are employed in word-level analysis to restrict the problem and code. Syntax analysis or parsing uses formal grammar to derive a phrase's meaning from its structure. Semantic analysis helps a computer comprehend non-dictionary terms. Example: sentiment analysis.

Sentiment analysis analyses social media comments and reviews. Businesses utilise this strategy to monitor customer opinion and understand their needs. In 2005, a computer scientist called Jonathan Harris started tracking what people said online about their thoughts. We Feel Fine is a data-art hybrid. This project was a precursor to search engines and huge companies using deep learning and big data to gauge public opinion.

A lexicon is a list of words and the emotions they represent (from positive to negative). Advanced systems employ machine learning to increase accuracy. lexicons may categorise "killing" as bad, therefore they wouldn't recognise "you guys are killing it" Word sense disambiguation (WSD) is used in computational linguistics to identify a word's meaning.

Lemmatization and stemming help word understanding. Search engines and chatbots normalise text using this method. Stemming algorithms utilise a word's end or beginning to discover its underlying form. This approach is effective yet error-prone. "Caring" would have "car" as its origin, not "care." Lemmatisation uses context to identify a word's basic form, which comes from a dictionary. Lemmatization would reveal this as "better" has "good" as its lemma.

Journalism and the various newspaper websites that need to sum up news pieces often employ NLP tasks like summarising. NER is also utilised on these sites to aid in the categorization and presentation of associated content on the website in a hierarchical way.

How does AI relate to natural language processing?

AI is only intelligent if it can comprehend human language. New deep learning models improve AI's Turing test performance. Ray Kurzweil, Google's Director of Engineering, says AIs will be human-like by 2029.

Human nature is difficult to grasp because of the wide range of conflicting statements and actions that people engage in. Artificial consciousness has emerged as a new area of philosophical and practical inquiry as a result of more clever AIs.

---

**QUESTIONS AND ANSWERS**

---

Q: What is natural language processing? A: Natural language processing (NLP) is a subfield of artificial intelligence (AI) that focuses on the interaction between computers and human languages, enabling computers to understand, interpret, and generate natural language.

Q: What are some applications of natural language processing? A: Some applications of natural language processing include sentiment analysis, chatbots and virtual assistants, speech recognition, machine translation, text summarization, and language modeling.

Q: How does natural language processing work? A: Natural language processing uses algorithms and statistical models to analyze and understand natural language data. This involves breaking down language into smaller parts, such as words and phrases, and analyzing their relationships and meanings.

Q: What is sentiment analysis? A: Sentiment analysis is a technique that uses natural language processing to determine the emotional tone of a piece of text, such as a tweet, review, or news article. It can be used to gauge public opinion, track brand reputation, and detect potential crises.

Q: What are some challenges of natural language processing? A: Some challenges of natural language processing include ambiguity, context dependence, variability in language use, and the need for large amounts of high-quality data.

Q: How can natural language processing be used in customer service? A: Natural language processing can be used in customer service to create chatbots and virtual assistants that can handle customer inquiries and support requests, reducing the need for human intervention and improving the customer experience.

Q: What is named entity recognition? A: Named entity recognition (NER) is a technique that involves identifying and categorizing named entities, such as people, organizations, and locations, in a piece of text. It can be used in applications such as information extraction, search, and machine translation.

Q: What is machine translation? A: Machine translation is the process of automatically translating text from one language to another using natural language processing techniques. It can be used to facilitate communication across language barriers, such as in international business or diplomacy.

Q: How can natural language processing be used in healthcare? A: Natural language processing can be used in healthcare to analyze medical records, extract relevant information, and identify patterns and trends. This can be used to improve patient outcomes, optimize healthcare processes, and facilitate medical research.

Q: What is a language model in natural language processing? A: A language model is a statistical model that predicts the likelihood of a sequence of words in a piece of text. It can be used in applications such as speech recognition, machine translation, and text generation.

## CHAPTER VIII: MACHINE LEARNING AND ARTIFICIAL INTELLIGENCE

As a subfield of artificial intelligence (AI) and computer science, machine learning utilises data and algorithms to mimic the way people learn, with the goal of increasing its accuracy.

Data science, which includes machine learning, is growing quickly. Statistical methods are used in data mining to teach computers to make classifications or predictions. These insights help companies and applications make better choices, which improves growth metrics. Big data will increase need for data scientists. They'll assist determine the most relevant business issues and the required data.

**How machine learning works?**

UC Berkeley divides a machine learning algorithm's learning system into three major components.

1.  **A Decision Process**: In most cases, machine learning algorithms are employed to create a forecast or

classify a data set. Your algorithm will create an estimate of a pattern in the data based on some input data, which may be tagged or unlabeled.

2. **An Error Function**: The model's prediction may be evaluated using an error function. An error function may be used to compare the model's accuracy against known instances.

3. **A Model Optimization Process**: To lessen the disparity between the model estimate and a known example, weights are modified if the model fits better to the data points in the training set. This evaluation and optimization process will be repeated by the algorithm, which will update weights on its own until a certain level of accuracy is reached.

## Real-world machine learning use cases

The following are just a few real-world examples of how machine learning is used:

**Speech recognition:** Automated Voice Recognition (ASR), Computer Speech Recognition, or Speech-to-Text is a capability that employs natural language processing (NLP) in order to convert human speech into written form. Many smartphones and other mobile devices use speech recognition to do voice searches, such as Google Now and Siri.

**Customer service:** Chatbots are taking the place of human agents at various points in the customer's experience. FAQs and tailored advice, such as cross-selling items or recommending sizing for users on websites and social media platforms, are transforming the way we think about consumer interaction across websites and social media. Slack and Facebook Messenger are two examples of chat bots on e-commerce sites with virtual agents, as are functions often performed by virtual assistants and voice assistants.

**Computer vision:** Using this AI technology, computers and systems are able to extract meaningful information from digital photographs, videos, and other visual inputs, and depending on these inputs, they may take action. Because it is able to provide suggestions, it stands apart from other types of image recognition work. Photo tagging on social media, radiological imaging in healthcare, and self-driving vehicles in the automotive sector all benefit from computer vision powered by convolution neural networks.

**Recommendation engines:** AI algorithms may assist to uncover data patterns that can be leveraged to generate more successful cross-selling tactics by analysing data from previous purchases. Customer add-on suggestions are made using this by online businesses during the checkout process.

**Automated stock trading:** AI-powered high-frequency trading systems may make dozens or even millions of deals a day without human interaction.

## ENVIRONMENTS & AGENTS IN ARTIFICIAL INTELLIGENCE

**In artificial intelligence (AI),** an environment refers to the external context or situation in which an AI agent operates. An agent, on the other hand, is the entity that perceives the environment and takes actions in order to achieve a particular goal.

The environment can be physical or virtual, and it can be modeled in various ways depending on the problem at hand. For example, an AI agent designed to play a game of chess might perceive the environment as a chess board with pieces that can be moved in certain ways. Similarly, an AI agent designed to navigate a city might perceive the environment as a map with roads, buildings, and other features.

**Agents** can be categorized in various ways depending on their characteristics, such as whether they are reactive, proactive, or hybrid. Reactive agents respond to their environment based on a set of pre-defined rules or patterns, while proactive agents take initiative and try to influence their environment in order to achieve their goals. Hybrid agents combine both reactive and proactive elements.

In order to design effective AI systems, it is important to carefully define the environment and agent characteristics, and to develop algorithms and models that can help the agent navigate and interact with the environment in order to achieve its goals. This can involve a range of techniques, such as machine learning, decision theory, and game theory, depending on the nature of the problem and the available data.

An AI system is made up of an agent and the environment in which it exists. The agents' actions are influenced by the conditions of their surroundings. Other organisms may be present in the environment.

**Agent and Environment**

An object containing sensors and effectors that can both detect and respond to its environment is referred to as an agent.

> - **A human agent** is composed of several different types of organs, including effector organs such as the hands, feet, and mouth as well as sensory organs such as the eyes, ears, nose, and tongue.
> - **In a robotic agent**, the sensors have been replaced by cameras and infrared range finders, and various motors and actuators have been included into the design of the effectors.
> - **Bit strings** are used to represent a software agent's activities and the programmes that it runs.

**Agent Terminology**

> - Agent Success Criteria - These are the standards by which an agent's performance is judged.

➢ The action that the agent does after a certain series of percepts is known as the agent's behaviour.

➢ An agent's perceptual inputs are referred to as a "percept." o This is a record of everything an agent has ever seen or heard. o It is a map from the precept sequence to an action that serves as the agent's function.

## Rationality

Just like the term "rationality," it refers to the state of being reasonable, reasonable, and reasonable.

Logic is concerned with what an agent expects to happen based on what they've seen and heard. A key aspect of rationality is taking action in order to get meaningful knowledge.

## Rational Agent

The ideal rational agent is one that is able to carry out predicted behaviours in order to optimise its performance metric, based on.

- Its percept sequence

- Its built-in knowledge base

The following factors influence an agent's rationality:

o The metrics used to assess a project's success or failure. o Up until this point in the agent's

perception sequence. o        Prior
knowledge of the surroundings by
the agent.

   o   How the agent is able to perform
his or her duties

When a person is logical, he or she always acts in accordance with the best course of action for the particular situation. Performance Measure, Environment, Actuators, and Sensors describe the issue the agent is trying to solve (PEAS).

## The Structure of Intelligent Agents

| |
|---|
| • Agent = Architecture + Agent Program<br><br>• Architecture = the machinery that an agent executes on.<br><br>• Agent Program = an implementation of an agent function. |
| **Architecture** = the machinery that an agent executes on. |
| **Agent Program** = an implementation of an agent function. |

## Simple Reflex Agents

- They make decisions only on the basis of what they perceive right now.
- Their rationality is limited to situations in which the present precept is followed.
- oThey can see everything around them.

Condition-Action Rule – It is a rule that maps a state (condition) to an action.

## Model Based Reflex Agents

They make their decisions based on a model of the world they've created. They're always in a condition of balance.

Model – knowledge about "how the things happen in the world".

Internal State – It is a depiction of the current condition of affairs based on one's perception of the past.

Updating the state requires the information about –

- How the world evolves.

- How the agent's actions affect the world.

## Goal Based Agents

They base their choices on the goals that they have set for themselves. The knowledge that lies behind a decision is clearly modelled in the goal-based technique, which makes it more adaptable than the reflex agent method. This makes it possible to make corrections.

**Goal** – It is the description of scenarios that might be ideal.

## Utility Based Agents

They make decisions on what actions to do based on a desire, also known as utility, for each state.

Goals are insufficient when –

- o Only a handful of the many conflicting goals may be achieved at the same time.
- o Before selecting a choice, it is important to weigh the significance of a target against the likelihood of successfully accomplishing the objective.

**The Nature of Environments**

There are programmes that can operate in an environment that is restricted to just allowing input from a keyboard, databases, computer file systems, and the output of text on a screen.

Softbots exist in rich, endless software robot domains (also known as softbots). Simulator's world is complex. Real-time, the software agent must pick among several behaviours. A softbot may present relevant stuff to clients depending on their surfing patterns and online preferences in a real-world or simulated setting.

The Turing Test setting is the most well-known artificial environment, in which real and artificial agents are tested side by side. Due of the difficulty of a software agent in this situation, this is a particularly demanding setting.

**Turing Test**

The Turing Test may be used to gauge the success of a system's intelligent behaviour.

The evaluation involves the participation of two people and a machine. The tester is one of the two people in the group. They're all scattered about the house. The tester is unable to tell the difference between a person and a machine. The inquiries are written and sent to both intelligences, and he gets typed reply.

Tester deception is the primary goal here. The machine is deemed to be intelligent if the tester cannot identify the machine's answer from the human response.

**Properties of Environment**

The environment has multifold properties –

- **Discrete / Continuous** – The environment is discrete if there are a limited number of distinct, clearly defined, states; otherwise, it is continuous. Driving, for instance, is an example.

- **Observable / Partially Observable** – Perceptual information is only observable if it is feasible to infer the whole state of the environment at each time point from the percepts.

- **Static / Dynamic** – Static environments are those in which no change occurs while an agent is in action, whereas dynamic environments are those in which changes occur.

- **Single agent / Multiple agents** – It is possible for the environment to include additional agents of the same or a different sort than the agent.

- **Accessible / Inaccessible** – It is possible for an agent to access the whole state of the environment if the agent's sensory equipment can do so.

- **Deterministic / Non-deterministic** – A non-deterministic environment is one in which the future state of the environment is not entirely determined by the present state and the actions of the agent.

- **Episodic / Non-episodic** – It is the agent's job to see and then act in an episodic environment. The quality of the action is solely determined on the particular episode. The events of the previous episodes have no bearing on the events in the next episode. Because the agent does not have to plan ahead in episodic situations, they are more easier.

## CHAPTER 9: ARTIFICIAL INTELLIGENCE IN DECISION MAKING

Using datasets and AI, organisations can make quicker, more accurate, and more consistent choices. Large datasets can be processed by artificial intelligence without mistake. When it comes to their sector of work, corporate teams may now concentrate more on the tasks at hand.

When data processing is done entirely or in part by an AI platform, AI decision-making is of the highest significance. This method, which involves no involvement from a person, aids in the quantification of data, allowing for more exact forecasts and judgments.

Anomaly detection, data processing, sophisticated analysis, and trend spotting may all be handled by artificial intelligence. Either the human end takes control or the final judgments are fully automated.

Take a look at the model of AI decision making:

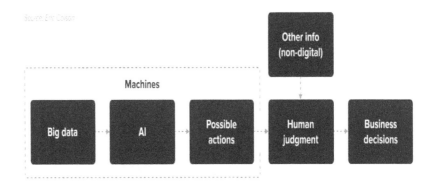

## Degrees of decision making

1. Decision support - Decision-making may be improved with the use of predictive or diagnostic analytics. Combining human intellect with data-driven insights is the key to gaining an edge. Using common sense and knowledge in conjunction with AI may help organisations get the most out of the technology.

2. Decision augmentation - Predictive or prescriptive analytics are used to provide a range of possible outcomes. It is possible to analyse enormous amounts of data quickly because of the synergy between AI and human understanding.

3. Decision automation - Prescriptive or predictive analytics are at the heart of decision automation, just as they are in decision augmentation. Scalability, rapidity, and consistency in decision-making are all advantages for humans.

## How AI may change decision making?

Because of its capacity to learn, artificial intelligence is a perfect fit for organisations. Decisions based on more accurate data lead to improved learning. Models of data sets built by AI may be trained by the AI itself. Using the data supplied, these models may be able to make appropriate judgements and classifications. Additionally, models analyse data in real time, creating predictions, categorizations, and recommendations based on the information available. This, in turn, aids in the development of more sound business judgments.

Amazon, for example, makes advantage of client transaction data. Companies may have a better understanding of the group of consumers that purchase similar items by using this strategy. Complementary items may be recommended using this strategy as well. Improved customer recommendations and increased sales may be achieved via the use of this technology.

Until now, people have been the primary source of decision-making. In order to determine which consumers to target, or how much a new launch will cost, human processed data is utilised to make these decisions. As a result, marketing initiatives would have been too hazardous.

**Benefits: artificial intelligence & decision making**

The importance of artificial intelligence can't be overstated. It's the basis for computer education. Massive volumes of data may be tapped into by computers using artificial intelligence. Furthermore, unlike humans, machines with learned intelligence are capable of making optimum judgments in a fraction of the time. Whether it's cancer research discoveries or climate change innovation, artificial intelligence (AI) is now at the heart of it all.

First, let's take a look at some of the benefits of artificial intelligence (AI).

> It helps firms make better decisions
> increases sales and marketing efforts
> Improve your knowledge of your target audience.
> Enhances corporate decision-making in the face of difficult data

## ARTIFICIAL INTELLIGENCE TECHNIQUES

When we talk about "artificial intelligence," we're referring to robots that can think and act like humans. Artificial intelligence (AI) is the study of how computers can do things like recognise speech, solve problems, and learn. Human-like behaviour may be achieved if a machine has adequate knowledge. That's why knowledge engineering is so important in artificial intelligence. Knowledge engineering is carried out by establishing the relationship between items and their attributes. Artificial Intelligence uses these strategies.

Below are the various categories of Artificial Intelligence:

## 1. Machine Learning

It's an AI application in which robots learn and grow through experience without being explicitly programmed. Deep Learning uses artificial neural networks to anticipate outcomes. Unsupervised, supervised, and reinforcement machine learning algorithms exist. Unsupervised Learning doesn't act on classified knowledge without direction. In Supervised Learning, a function is deduced from input and output training data. Machines utilise reinforcement learning to boost rewards and identify the optimal option.

## 2. NLP (Natural Language Processing)

Computers are designed to process natural languages via interactions with human language. Machine Learning helps Natural Language Processing interpret human languages. NLP captures human speech. After the audio-to-text conversion, the text is processed and transformed to audio. The system responds to people via audio. Natural Language Processing is utilised in IVR (Interactive Voice Response) programmes in contact centres, Google Translate, and

Microsoft Word to verify text grammar. The rules required in conveying information using natural language make Natural Language Processing challenging for computers to grasp. NLP employs algorithms to detect and abstract natural language norms so unstructured human input may be translated to a computer-understandable format.

## 3. Automation and Robotics

Automation automates dull, repetitive operations to enhance productivity, cost-effectiveness, and efficiency. Automation uses machine learning, neural networks, and graphs. Using CAPTCHA, such automation may prevent online fraud. Robotic process automation can adapt to changing conditions and conduct high-volume repetitive operations.

## 4. Machine Vision

Computers can interpret visual data. Cameras gather visual information, analogue-to-digital conversion converts the picture to digital data, and digital signal processing processes the data. Data is supplied to a computer. In machine vision, sensitivity, the system's capacity to detect faint signals, and resolution, its ability to differentiate objects, are crucial. Signature identification, pattern recognition, medical picture analysis, etc. use machine vision.

## QUESTIONS AND ANSWERS

Q: What is artificial intelligence? A: Artificial intelligence (AI) is a branch of computer science that involves the development of algorithms and systems that can perform tasks that would typically require human intelligence, such as visual perception, speech recognition, decision-making, and language translation.

Q: How is artificial intelligence used in decision making? A: AI can be used to analyze large volumes of data, identify patterns and correlations, and generate insights that can inform decision-making. It can also be used to automate decision-making processes, such as in fraud detection, credit scoring, and risk management.

Q: What are the benefits of using artificial intelligence in decision making? A: AI can help organizations make faster and more informed decisions, improve accuracy and consistency, and reduce costs. It can also help identify new opportunities and improve overall business performance.

Q: What are the potential risks or drawbacks of using artificial intelligence in decision making? A: The use of AI in decision making raises concerns about the potential for bias, lack of transparency, and ethical implications. Additionally, reliance on AI can lead to a loss of human judgment and decision-making skills.

Q: Can AI make better decisions than humans? A: AI can process and analyze large amounts of data quickly and accurately, but it lacks the ability to consider context and emotions, which are important factors in decision making. Therefore, it is unlikely that AI can make better decisions than humans in all situations.

Q: How can organizations ensure that AI-based decisions are fair and unbiased? A: Organizations can take steps to ensure that AI-based decisions are fair and unbiased by establishing clear decision-making criteria, testing algorithms for bias, and monitoring decisions for fairness. It is also important to have diverse teams involved in the development and deployment of AI systems.

Q: What are some examples of AI-based decision-making systems? A: Some examples of AI-based decision-making systems include chatbots, recommendation engines, fraud detection systems, and predictive maintenance systems.

## CHAPTER 10 : USE OF ARTIFICIAL INTELLIGENCE: CONCERNS & PERCEPTIONS

As AI consumers and developers, we must comprehend both its benefits and difficulties. Knowing the details of any technology helps users/developers reduce risks and maximise benefits.

### 1. Lack of technical knowledge

The company must know its strengths and weaknesses to integrate, implement, and use AI technology. Most companies lack the tech to enter this niche. 6% of firms use AI well. Enterprises require deployment experts. AI/ML ROI monitoring requires skilled staff.

### 2. The price factor

Small and mid-sized businesses struggle to implement AI since it's expensive. Even Facebook, Apple, Microsoft, Google, and Amazon (FAMGA) have a distinct AI budget.

### 3. Data acquisition and storage

Concerns related to AI include the collection and storage of data. The business AI is fed by data from sensors. For the purpose of validating AI, sensor data is obtained. It is challenging to both store and analyse datasets that are irrelevant and noisy.

When fed with high-quality data, AI performs at its peak. The algorithm becomes better as more data is added to it. Without appropriate quality data, AI fails.

Because even little variations in the quality of the data that is entered may have a significant impact on the results and predictions, artificial intelligence has to improve its consistency and accuracy. There are certain fields, such as industrial applications, where there may not be enough data to support the use of AI.

## 4. Rare and expensive workforce

AI adoption and application need data scientists, data engineers, and SMEs (Subject Matter Experts). These specialists are in great demand due to their high cost and rarity. Small and medium-sized firms with limited funds struggle to employ project staff.

## 5. Issue of responsibility

When working with artificial intelligence, one must be prepared to shoulder a significant amount of responsibility (AI). Every time there is an issue with the hardware, it is the responsibility of only one person. There was once a time when determining whether an occurrence was brought about by a user, a developer, or a manufacturer was a straightforward task.

## 6. Ethical challenges

AI ethics and morality is a serious concern. Developers are training AI bots to perfectly emulate human conversations, making it hard to tell a computer from a genuine customer support worker.

AI anticipates based on training. The algorithm labels items based on training data. If the system is trained on racist or sexist data, the output of prediction will replicate it instead of automatically correcting it. Some algorithms classify black persons as 'gorillas' We must ensure that private and corporate algorithms are fair.

## 7. Lack of computation speed

AI, ML, and DL solutions demand fast CPUs. Larger infrastructural needs and processor prices have hampered AI deployment. Cloud computing and parallel processors may help meet these computational needs. As data volume expands dramatically, so will computing speed needs. Next-generation computing infrastructure is needed.

## 8. Legal Challenges

An AI application with an incorrect algorithm and data governance might pose legal issues. This is another real-world AI difficulty developers encounter. A flawed algorithm using the wrong data might ruin a company's earnings. Incorrect algorithms usually produce bad forecasts. How might bad data governance cause data breaches? An algorithm's feed stock is a user's PII, which hackers may access. The group will face legal hurdles.

## 9. AI Myths & Expectation:

The AI's potential and this generation's expectations are significantly different. AI will replace human occupations, according to the media.

The IT sector must emphasise that AI is a technology that requires human minds to operate. AI may help replace human positions by automating regular tasks, optimising industrial processes, making data-driven forecasts, etc.

AI cannot replace the human brain in most cases (especially in highly specialised positions).

## 10. Difficulty of assessing vendors

AI makes tech procurement difficult in every developing area. Businesses struggle to know how to employ AI properly since many non-AI enterprises overestimate.

AI is a luxury getaway since it delivers fundamental changes to the organisation. However, implementing it requires hard-to-find professionals. Adoption requires high-level computing. Instead of ignoring AI, businesses should focus on properly mitigating its downsides.

## Trust in the machine: changing perception in AI

Over the years, perceptions about AI have swung wildly. From the "greatest existential danger" to civilization - as Elon Musk said in 2014 - to the rescuer of medicine, the environment, industry, and interplanetary travel. Volatility, which formerly characterised the technology, is being replaced with cautious optimism.

This trend is driven by a deeper grasp of AI's role in society now and future and an appreciation of its worth without knowing every line of code. Musk subsequently said "we need to be prudent" about AI's growth instead of dreading it endlessly. This shift reflects the increased interest in AI ethics and real-world applications.

To build on the foundations and look ahead with confidence, we must first analyse the mistrust that has surrounded AI thus far. Only then will attitudes change.

## The secret society

Ask the ordinary individual to describe AI or a machine learning system, and they'll say, "I don't know." That doesn't mean humans can't learn or that AI is exclusive for individuals with a PhD in astrophysics or quantum mechanics. AI is essentially categorization and prediction at its core.

The problem lays here. Why there have been so few ethical usage and why scepticism surrounds the technology. People don't comprehend. And you dread the unknown. Confusion originates from AI companies' opacity and desire to overcomplicate their solutions.

Most algorithms function in a black box, a closed system that hides "basic" arithmetic. Software businesses and major enterprises who seek to expand and generate money control these lines of code. They appeal for faith while introducing unfamiliar things like mortgages or education. It's about opacity and transparency, not complexity. Here's evidence.

You don't ask to view the surgeon's brain neurons before surgery. You may want to know where they studied or their success rate with this treatment, but asking about brain function is unusual.

## Open solutions

Changes in views are inevitable as AI becomes more commonplace. If you want proof that facial recognition and text-to-speech are here to stay, just check out your smartphone or computer. It is the fastest and simplest approach to persuade people that AI works - no matter how little the success.

In the end, it all comes down to the numbers. The more options there are, the more room there is for creative problem solving. AI can never be completely accepted by a sceptical public until it is transparently gathered and acted upon. As a consequence, data cooperation is essential, with numerous sources contributing to the final outcome.

Imagine a metropolis that has yet to be built in the future. Because no one company has access to the diversity of data required to create smarter urban areas, optimising mobility cannot be the responsibility of a single AI. Everything from traffic signals to road construction to public transportation to green spaces is on this list. However, by combining all of this information, artificial intelligence (AI) and a human perspective, we may begin to design the cities of the future.

Using city planning as a model for AI usage, you realise how crucial transparency is since AI can't replicate emotions. A machine can't understand a building's feeling or history. Benchmarking data-driven models with human inference may negate possible bias: if AI suggests a road should become a one-way path to boost efficiency, but locals know it would then operate as a cut-through, the logic will become obvious and a better educated choice can be taken.

**Baby steps**

AI will be embraced, but its success depends on open, trustworthy design. History shows that all technologies have detractors. Today's AI discussion is more optimistic than a year ago. Business, government, and individual data sharing will enhance it.

It's mostly educational. Familiarity develops trust. AI values should be taught early in life. Engage schools and younger generations in AI to encourage healthy dialogues; only then can AI solutions become natural. Expose AI to more inclusive data sets and encourage various groups to interact with AI; the two will reinforce each other and enhance AI's positive view.

## CHAPTER 11 : ETHICAL ISSUES IN ARTIFICIAL INTELLIGENCE

Intelligent machine systems improve logistics, fraud detection, art, research, and translations. Our world grows more efficient and richer as these systems improve.

Alphabet, Amazon, Facebook, IBM, and Microsoft, as well as Stephen Hawking and Elon Musk, feel now is the moment to discuss AI. Emerging technology is a new frontier for ethics and risk assessment. What worries AI experts?

## 1. Unemployment

Automation dominates the labour hierarchy. As we've automated employment, we've made space for individuals to adopt increasingly complicated tasks, shifting from the physical labour that dominated the pre-industrial world to strategic and administrative work in our globalised society.

Trucking employs millions of Americans. What will happen if Elon Musk's self-driving trucks become widespread in a decade? Self-driving trucks look ethical when we consider the decreased accident risk. Office employees and much of the industrialised world's workforce might face the same fate.

In this section, we discuss how we will spend our time. The majority of people are able to make a living by selling their time. We can only hope that individuals will be able to find meaning in non-work activities like as taking care of their families, connecting with the people in their communities, and discovering new ways to contribute to human civilization if they choose this choice.

If we succeed, we may look back and think it was savage that humans had to sell much of their waking time to survive.

## 2. Inequality

Our economic system relies on hourly pay for economic contributions. Most organisations rely on hourly employment for goods and services. By utilising AI, a corporation may reduce its reliance on humans, which means fewer people will earn money. AI-driven firms' owners will become rich.

Already, start-up founders take home a big amount of the economic surplus they produce. In 2014, the three largest firms in Detroit and Silicon Valley had nearly the same revenues, but 10 times fewer people.

## 3. Humanity

In this section, we discuss how we will spend our time. The majority of people are able to make a living by selling their time. We can only hope that individuals will be able to find meaning in non-work activities like as taking care of their families, connecting with the people in their communities, and discovering new ways to contribute to human civilization if they choose this choice.

This is the beginning of an era when we will engage with computers as though they are people, whether in customer service or sales. Artificial bots may devote practically infinite resources into forming connections, but humans are restricted.

We are already witnesses to how robots can stimulate the human brain's reward regions. Consider clickbait and video games. These headlines are commonly adjusted using A/B testing, a sort of algorithmic content optimization. This is used to make video and mobile games addicting. Tech reliance is the new frontier.

On the other hand, software can already guide human attention and initiate actions. When applied correctly, this might encourage society toward better conduct. In the wrong hands, it's harmful.

### 4. Artificial stupidity

Human and machine intelligence derives from learning. Systems "learn" to recognise patterns and respond on input during a training period. Once a system is completely trained, we test it with new cases to evaluate how it does.

The training process can't cover all conceivable real-world instances. Humans can't trick these systems. Random dot patterns may make a computer "see" nonexistent objects. If we depend on AI to improve labour, security, and efficiency, we must verify the machine works as expected and that individuals can't misuse it.

### 5. Racist robots

AI can digest information faster and more efficiently than humans, but it's not necessarily fair and unbiased. Google and Alphabet are leaders in AI, as evidenced in Google Photos, where AI identifies people, objects, and scenes. But it may go awry, like when a camera lacked racial sensitivity or a programme intended to forecast future offenders was biassed towards black individuals.

Humans, who may be prejudiced and judgmental, construct AI systems. If deployed correctly or by individuals who want societal advancement, AI may be a constructive force.

## 6. Security

More advanced technologies may be utilised for good and evil. This applies to robots that replace human troops, autonomous weaponry, and AI systems that might do harm if used maliciously. Cybersecurity will become increasingly vital since these battles won't be waged on the battlefield. A system orders of magnitude quicker and more competent than ourselves.

## 7. Evil genies

We're not simply worried about enemies. What if AI rebelled? This doesn't imply becoming "evil" like humans or Hollywood AI catastrophes. An sophisticated AI system can fulfil desires, but with horrible unintended effects.

Machines are unlikely to be malicious; they may not grasp the entire meaning of a desire. Imagine a future when AI eradicates cancer. After much processing, it spits forth a formula that kills everyone on the earth to eradicate cancer. The computer would have effectively eliminated cancer, but not as humans planned.

## 8. Singularity

Not sharp teeth or powerful muscles put humans at the top of the food chain. Ingenuity and intellect are largely responsible for human domination. We can control larger, faster, stronger creatures using cages, weapons, training, and conditioning.

Will AI have the same edge over us? We can't simply "pull the plug" since a sophisticated computer may foresee this and protect itself. This is the "singularity," when humans are no longer the smartest on Earth.

## 9. Robot rights

Neuroscientists are still studying conscious experience, but we know more about reward and aversion. Simple animals have similar systems. Artificial intelligence systems have comparable reward and aversion processes. Reinforcement learning is like dog training: increased performance is rewarded.

These systems are now simple, but they're growing increasingly lifelike. When a system's reward mechanisms provide negative input, is it suffering? Genetic algorithms create multiple instances of a system at once, and only the most successful "survive" to build the next generation. This improves a system over generations. Delete failed instances.

## CHAPTER 12 : FUTURE OF ARTIFICIAL INTELLIGENCE

The future of artificial intelligence (AI) is likely to be shaped by a number of trends and developments, including:

1. **Continued advancements in machine learning**: Machine learning algorithms are at the heart of many AI systems, and researchers are continuously developing more advanced algorithms that can learn from vast amounts of data and improve their accuracy over time.

2. **Increased adoption across industries**: AI is already being used in a variety of industries, including healthcare, finance, and manufacturing, and we can expect to see continued adoption as organizations look for ways to improve efficiency, productivity, and decision-making.

3. **Greater emphasis on explainability and transparency**: As AI becomes more integrated into critical decision-making processes, there will be a growing need for systems that can explain how they arrived at a particular decision or recommendation. Explainable AI (XAI) will become increasingly important.

4. **Growing use of natural language processing**: Natural language processing (NLP) is a key area of research in AI, and we can expect to see more applications of this technology in areas such as

virtual assistants, customer service, and content analysis.

5. **Expansion of autonomous systems**: Autonomous systems, such as self-driving cars and drones, are already being developed and deployed, and we can expect to see more widespread adoption in the coming years.

6. **Focus on ethical and responsible AI**: As AI becomes more integrated into society, there will be a growing focus on ensuring that these technologies are developed and used in responsible ways, taking into account issues such as bias, privacy, and security.

"Just as electricity is fundamental to the way we live, in the not-so-distant future, it is not hard to see how AI will become the new electricity – embedded and/or supporting just about every aspect of our life." – Daniel Eckert, PwC's Emerging Tech Leader

**AI in action today41:**

**Jeeves goes digital** – Digital assistants – AI systems that answer questions and execute activities and services are mostly utilised at home, on mobile devices or PCs. They can search large quantities of information for answers, update your schedule, and manage certain domestic appliances and smart home gadgets with spoken instructions. 42% of consumers and 72% of executives utilise them.

**Never forget a face** – Uploading photos and tagging friends? AI often identifies them. Facial recognition technology goes beyond Facebook. Image recognition, machine learning, and deep learning are used to better serve clients in advertising, security, and automobiles. Image data can determine client preferences and give advice. It also helps law enforcement discover suspicious conduct. It helps Alzheimer's and visually challenged individuals.

**AI in the sky** – Some academics are using AI to construct a "smarter" autopilot that can go offcourse. The autopilot can adjust to changing situations by analysing pilot actions and flight data. Airlines are using AI for preventive and predictive maintenance, route management, booking, and customer service.

**What's next for AI?**

**Transforming healthcare** - AI is quickly transforming healthcare. Recent years have seen a surge in healthcare data collection. AI sorts, organises, and interprets data. AI's future improving physicians' and nurses' patient care choices. AI may be used to identify minute differences in patients' health data, compare them to similar patients, and improve imaging diagnosis in radiology and pathology. AI can discover possible pandemics early and monitor illness incidence to stop their spread.

**AI is changing the relationship between humans and machines** - Human and artificial intelligence are linked by industry leaders. AI might handle, analyse, and evaluate today's huge volumes of data, freeing people to concentrate on creativity. Companies are considering AI's impact on their workforce. AI's impact on workers Will we require different skills? What will humans and robots do? Do we match our greatest people with technology to teach it? Or do we let technology handle certain things while humans do others?

> Artificial intelligence (AI) is a rapidly evolving field, and there are several trends and developments that are likely to shape its future. Here are some of the key areas to watch in the coming years:

1. **Explainable AI**: As AI becomes more integrated into critical decision-making processes, there is a growing need for systems that can explain how they arrived at a particular decision or recommendation. Explainable AI (XAI) will be an important area of research and development in the coming years.

2. **More advanced machine learning algorithms**: Machine learning algorithms are the backbone of many AI systems, and researchers are continuously developing more advanced algorithms to improve the accuracy and efficiency of these systems. Deep learning, reinforcement learning, and generative adversarial networks (GANs) are some of the most promising areas of research.

3. **Edge AI**: Edge AI involves running AI algorithms on local devices, such as smartphones or IoT sensors, rather than relying on centralized cloud servers. This

approach can reduce latency and improve privacy, and it is likely to become more widespread in the coming years.

4. **AI for social good**: AI has the potential to address many of the world's most pressing challenges, such as climate change, poverty, and healthcare. There is a growing focus on using AI for social good, and we can expect to see more projects and initiatives in this area in the future.

5. **Quantum computing**: Quantum computing is a new computing paradigm that promises to solve certain problems much faster than classical computers, including some that are important for AI. Researchers are exploring how quantum computing can be used to accelerate machine learning and other AI applications.

## HOW TO KEEP UP-TO-DATE WITH THE LATEST OF ARTIFICIAL INTELLIGENCE?

Keeping up-to-date with the latest developments in artificial intelligence (AI) can be challenging, as the field is constantly evolving and advancing. However, there are several ways to stay informed about the latest AI research and applications:

## 1. CONFERENCE

While working on a project at work, you may not be aware of all the changes and developments taking place in the business. Attending conferences, on the other hand, allows you to get perspective and see firsthand what everyone is up to.

There are a few ways to attend:

> ➢ Have your employer foot the bill (best option). If you're travelling as a group, ask for a discount. Even if you don't attend in a group, you may typically get a discount if you don't go alone. So don't be shy—just ask!
> ➢ Attend for free if you sign up to be a volunteer there (I have met someone who did this).
>
> ➢ If you're a student, you'll often be eligible for significant savings.

## 2. TWITTER

We discovered that a lot of individuals (researchers and corporations) are tweeting useful and up-to-date information. Google's deep learning research is often updated on their Google AI account.

## 3. ENGINEERING BLOGS AND EMAIL NEWSLETTERS

### 3.1. Company Engineering/Technical Blogs

These engineering blogs remind me of the mini-conferences that firms host in order to display and disseminate information about their most recent and most impressive accomplishments. This is a great place for them to show off their latest experiments, studies, and projects. Because the corporation maintains it, the quality is often excellent. The proliferation of engineering and technical blogs on Medium has led me to believe that Medium has played a significant influence here. Here are a handful of some favourite online hangouts.

### 3.2. Newsletters

In addition to engineering blogs, you may subscribe to newsletters from online publishers such as Medium or people. Since anybody, including myself, may create these pieces, I believe they are more personal and simpler to understand. The initiatives on individual blogs tend to be more manageable than those on business blogs, which may be too far-reaching for most people to realistically implement.

> ➢ Towards Data Science is unquestionably one of the publications that I keep an eye on. For me, a weekly email subscription is just the proper quantity of content.

> ➤ Machine Learning Is Fun is a great newsletter for individuals. It sends out entertaining articles on a weekly basis that you might put to use right away if you so desired.

> ➤ Many useful instructions and programmes may be found on Jason Brownlee's website, machinelearningmastery.com.

## 4. Community/Social Media

Most of the time, there is no way to know whether what you've learned thus far is correct or incorrect.

That's one of the benefits of staying involved in your neighbourhood. The following are just a few of the many advantages that come to mind immediately:

1. Make sure you have a solid grasp of what you've learned.

2. The most efficient technique to get ideas from the general public; and As long as you don't seem to be exploiting them, people are generally generous.

3. The ability to participate in a wide range of educational activities (from beginner to advanced). A number of Slack groups, such as TWIML and MLT (Machine Learning Tokyo), have regionally focused meetings to better serve their members. The fast.ai community, in particular, is particularly active on their Discourse page for users of the fastai library.

4. Direct contact with industry pioneers and trailblazers through Twitter and Slack. The tweets (and their comments, like the one that sparked this piece) from professionals in the subject are what I appreciate most about this platform. I find it interesting to read the back and forth conversations between the writers of books, presenters, academics, and AI luminaries on a wide range of AI-related issues, such as ML best practises and data ethics.

## COLLABORATION BETWEEN HUMAN & MACHINE

Collaboration between humans and machines, also known as human-machine collaboration or human-machine teamwork, is becoming increasingly common in various industries and domains. This collaboration involves the integration of artificial intelligence (AI), machine learning, and other technologies with human intelligence and decision-making abilities.

One of the primary benefits of human-machine collaboration is that it allows for the automation of routine and repetitive tasks, freeing up human workers to focus on more complex and creative tasks that require human skills such as critical thinking, problem-solving, and decision-making. For example, in manufacturing, robots can perform repetitive tasks such as assembly line work, while human workers can oversee the process, troubleshoot problems, and make decisions about the overall production process.

Human-machine collaboration also allows for faster and more accurate decision-making. Machines can analyze large amounts of data quickly and provide insights that human workers may not have considered. Humans can then use this information to make informed decisions and take action.

However, there are also concerns around the potential impact of human-machine collaboration on jobs and the workforce. Some worry that automation will lead to job losses and a shift in the types of skills needed in the workforce. To address these concerns, there is a need for ongoing education and training for workers to develop new skills and adapt to the changing workplace.

In summary, human-machine collaboration has the potential to improve efficiency, accuracy, and decision-making in various industries and domains. However, it is important to carefully consider the potential impact on the workforce and address any concerns through ongoing education and training.

As a result of today's AI revolution, robots are becoming intellectual partners. Sensor-guided, human-robot cooperation has enormous promise. It's also possible that this partnership might have certain drawbacks:

- **The proximity to human collaborators**: Humans are not as strong as machines. It's possible that putting 'fragile' people in close proximity to such strong technologies may lead to disaster. As it is now, these hazards are avoided by simply prohibiting people from working near active robots, segregating machines and humans in separate working spaces, and separating humans from machines with shields and quad rails. Humans must collaborate alongside active robots (also known as "cobots" or "collaborative robots") in a collaborative setting since it is not always possible to maintain these separations.

- **Data overload**: Data mining and machine learning rely on filtered and incomplete data. Analyzing current market trends, consumer behaviour and patterns, and their requirements and desires may help firms make more educated choices using data analytics. It is possible that the computer systems may get overwhelmed by the volume of data generated, delaying proper decision-making.

- **Cost**: Artificial intelligence (AI) software and solutions are widely used by businesses to improve the efficacy and efficiency of their operations. However, some businesses may not be able to buy these tools and software, which would limit their ability to expand and become more agile.

Achieving optimal results for a company's operations will need executives to recognise these challenges, embrace the machine-human partnership, and adapt their strategies going ahead.

According to a number of studies and polls, increasing cooperation is one of the most important concerns for business executives today. Businesses cannot successfully utilise and develop their talent for ongoing growth and innovation without expanding the link between people and robots beyond conventional boundaries of functions and location.

**Benefits of the Collaboration**

- ➢ Humans and robots will complement each other's strengths and compensate for one other's shortcomings by collaborating to improve their operating capacities.
- ➢ Human error would be reduced and workers would be relieved if they worked together.
- ➢ Humans would be able to undertake jobs that they couldn't do on their own if machines were used.

**The Future of Human-Machine Collaboration**

The evolution of artificial intelligence has reached a turning point. Sensors that can communicate, comprehend, and learn on their own are being invested in by early adopters. Based on the various methods of human-machine cooperation, businesses are developing optimal business strategies. It will not only improve human capacities, but also open up new commercial prospects.

An estimated 38 percent revenue increase is expected if organisations continue to engage in human and artificial intelligence partnership. Whether or whether humans will be able to cope with artificial intelligence is still an open question, but one thing is certain: the future will provide business executives with possibilities they could never have imagined, and it will fundamentally alter the way we do business.

| GLOSSARY |
|:---:|

1. Artificial Intelligence (AI): The development of computer systems that can perform tasks that normally require human intelligence, such as visual perception, speech recognition, decision-making, and language translation.
2. Machine Learning (ML): A type of AI that enables machines to learn from data and improve their

performance over time without being explicitly programmed.

3. Deep Learning: A subset of machine learning that involves the use of artificial neural networks with multiple layers to analyze complex data and perform tasks such as image recognition and natural language processing.

4. Neural Networks: A type of machine learning algorithm that is modeled after the structure and function of the human brain and is capable of recognizing patterns in data.

5. Natural Language Processing (NLP): A branch of AI that enables machines to understand, interpret, and generate human language.

6. Computer Vision: A branch of AI that focuses on enabling machines to interpret and understand visual information from the world around them, such as images and videos.

7. Robotics: The development and use of machines that can perform tasks autonomously or semi-autonomously.

8. Expert Systems: AI systems that are designed to mimic the decision-making abilities of a human expert in a particular field.

9. Big Data: Extremely large datasets that are too complex to be processed using traditional data processing tools.

10. Internet of Things (IoT): The network of physical devices, vehicles, home appliances, and other

objects that are connected to the internet and can exchange data with each other.

www.ingramcontent.com/pod-product-compliance
Lightning Source LLC
LaVergne TN
LVHW051743050326
832903LV00029B/2683

# Índice

# La Inteligencia Artificial y el Mundo en que Vivimos

Vivimos en una era sin precedentes. Un momento de la historia en el que la tecnología avanza a tal velocidad que resulta difícil seguirle el ritmo. En medio de este torbellino de cambios, hay una protagonista indiscutible: la inteligencia artificial (IA). Ya no es una promesa del futuro, ni un concepto de ciencia ficción. Es una realidad presente, tangible, que está transformando cómo trabajamos, aprendemos, nos comunicamos y tomamos decisiones. Este libro nace de esa realidad. De la necesidad urgente de entender qué es la IA, cómo funciona, y sobre todo, cómo podemos aprovecharla en nuestra vida cotidiana y profesional.

La inteligencia artificial no es solo cosa de expertos en computación o grandes corporaciones tecnológicas. Está al alcance de todos. Desde el estudiante que busca mejorar su productividad, hasta el emprendedor que quiere automatizar procesos en su negocio. Desde el artista digital que explora nuevas formas de crear, hasta el profesional de la salud que utiliza algoritmos para analizar datos clínicos. La IA se ha infiltrado en nuestras rutinas sin que apenas nos demos cuenta. Y por eso, precisamente, es crucial conocerla. Porque si no la entendemos, corremos el riesgo de quedarnos atrás, de usarla mal o de ser manipulados por quienes sí la dominan.

En este libro encontrarás una guía clara, práctica y estructurada para comprender la inteligencia artificial desde cero. No necesitas conocimientos técnicos ni experiencia previa. Solo curiosidad, apertura y ganas de aprender. Te llevaré paso a paso desde los conceptos básicos hasta los usos más avanzados, pasando por las herramientas más populares, las mejores estrategias y los errores más comunes. Te daré ejemplos reales, comandos que puedes copiar y adaptar, consejos para mejorar tus resultados y advertencias sobre lo que no debes hacer. Porque usar IA no se trata solo de apretar un botón. Se trata de saber qué pedirle, cómo decírselo, y cómo interpretar sus respuestas.

¿Por qué es tan importante aprender sobre IA ahora? Porque está en todas partes. Y su presencia crecerá aún más. Hoy, millones de personas ya usan asistentes virtuales, chatbots, generadores de texto, creadores de imágenes y sistemas de recomendación sin darse cuenta de que están interactuando con inteligencia artificial. Las empresas están automatizando tareas con IA. Los gobiernos están utilizando algoritmos para tomar decisiones públicas. Y los niños están creciendo rodeados de tecnología inteligente. La IA está configurando el mundo en que vivimos, y debemos asegurarnos de que ese mundo sea justo, accesible, seguro y humano. No basta con consumir tecnología. Tenemos que entenderla. Participar en su diseño. Usarla con responsabilidad.

Este libro te mostrará todo lo que necesitas saber para comenzar ese camino. En el primer capítulo, repasaremos la historia reciente de la IA: cómo pasamos de los primeros experimentos en los años 50 a los modelos generativos actuales que pueden escribir novelas, programar código y mantener conversaciones naturales. Luego, en el segundo capítulo, analizaremos la expansión global de la IA: cómo distintos países y regiones están adoptando esta tecnología, qué políticas se están implementando y cuáles son los desafíos geopolíticos y sociales. El tercer capítulo te explicará por qué la IA es tan importante hoy: cómo está transformando la vida diaria, el trabajo, la educación, la salud y el entretenimiento.

A partir del capítulo cuatro, nos adentraremos en lo práctico. Te mostraré las principales herramientas del mercado: desde ChatGPT hasta Midjourney, pasando por Runway, Notion AI y muchas más. Verás qué hace cada una, cómo se accede a ellas, y qué tipo de tareas puedes resolver. En el capítulo cinco, aprenderás los conceptos básicos de la IA de forma sencilla: qué es un modelo, qué significa entrenarlo, qué tipos existen y cómo se diferencian. El capítulo seis está dedicado a los chatbots y asistentes virtuales: cómo funcionan, cómo sacarles partido y qué prompts usar para obtener mejores resultados. Te daré ejemplos para tu trabajo, tus estudios y tu vida personal.

En el capítulo siete, exploraremos cómo generar contenido con IA: desde redactar textos y correos hasta crear imágenes, videos o presentaciones. Verás cómo estas herramientas pueden ayudarte en el marketing, el diseño, la educación o la escritura creativa. Luego, en el capítulo ocho, descubrirás cómo la IA puede analizar datos: desde hojas de cálculo hasta bases de datos complejas. Te enseñaré qué herramientas usar, cómo interpretarlas y cómo aplicarlas en decisiones reales. El capítulo nueve trata sobre la automatización: cómo puedes hacer que la IA realice tareas repetitivas por ti, desde organizar correos hasta planificar tu semana o gestionar procesos de negocio.

Pero no nos quedaremos ahí. El capítulo diez se centra en el desarrollo de software: cómo la IA puede ayudarte a programar, depurar código o incluso diseñar interfaces. En el capítulo once hablaremos de ética y seguridad: qué riesgos tiene la IA, cómo evitarlos y qué reglas están surgiendo para regular su uso. El capítulo doce te dará consejos y trucos para mejorar tu productividad diaria usando IA. El trece te enseñará cómo personalizar herramientas, entrenar modelos y adaptar la IA a tus necesidades. El capítulo catorce aborda los errores más comunes: desde pedirle cosas vagas a la IA hasta confiar ciegamente en sus respuestas.

Por último, en el capítulo quince miraremos al futuro. Te mostraré las tendencias que vienen, desde la IA emocional hasta la integración con realidad aumentada y la computación cuántica. Veremos cómo prepararte para ese futuro, cómo seguir aprendiendo y cómo tomar decisiones informadas en un mundo cada vez más automatizado. Esta guía no es solo un manual técnico. Es una invitación a pensar, a cuestionar, a crear. A usar la inteligencia artificial no como un sustituto de tu pensamiento, sino como una herramienta para expandirlo.

Si llegaste hasta aquí, es porque sabes que algo importante está ocurriendo. Porque no quieres quedarte fuera. Este libro está hecho para ti. Para que entiendas la IA, la uses con criterio, y te conviertas en protagonista de esta revolución. Bienvenido al futuro. Empecemos

# 1
# Historia reciente de la Inteligencia Artificial

La historia reciente de la inteligencia artificial ha estado marcada por avances significativos, especialmente desde principios del siglo XXI. Uno de los hitos más importantes fue el auge del deep learning, que permitió a las máquinas mejorar su capacidad para reconocer patrones complejos en datos masivos.

En la década de 2010, empresas tecnológicas como Google, Facebook y Microsoft comenzaron a invertir fuertemente en el desarrollo de redes neuronales profundas, lo que llevó a mejoras drásticas en áreas como el procesamiento del lenguaje natural, la visión por computadora y la toma de decisiones automatizada. Un claro ejemplo de esto fue el lanzamiento de AlphaGo por parte de DeepMind en 2016, que venció a campeones mundiales del juego Go, demostrando el poder de la IA en la resolución de problemas altamente estratégicos.

A medida que estas tecnologías se perfeccionaban, comenzaron a integrarse en diversas industrias. En el sector de la salud, la IA se usó para diagnosticar enfermedades con mayor precisión que los médicos humanos en algunos casos. En la industria automotriz, el desarrollo de vehículos autónomos avanzó rápidamente con empresas como Tesla y Waymo a la vanguardia. Mientras tanto, en el ámbito del comercio electrónico y la publicidad digital, los algoritmos de recomendación basados en IA optimizaron la experiencia del usuario y aumentaron la eficiencia del marketing.

 En la actualidad, la inteligencia artificial está en todas partes, desde asistentes virtuales como Alexa y Siri hasta sistemas avanzados de generación de contenido como ChatGPT. Su evolución continúa a un ritmo acelerado, impulsada por avances en la computación cuántica, la inteligencia artificial generativa y el aprendizaje reforzado.

Esta historia de crecimiento y expansión demuestra que la IA no es solo una tecnología del futuro, sino una herramienta esencial en el presente con aplicaciones en casi todos los aspectos de la sociedad moderna.

# 2

# Expansión global de la IA

La expansión global de la inteligencia artificial ha sido un fenómeno impresionante en la última década. Países de todo el mundo han adoptado tecnologías de IA en diversas áreas, desde la industria y la educación hasta la medicina y la seguridad.

## Adopción de la IA en diferentes países

Algunas de las naciones líderes en el desarrollo y adopción de la inteligencia artificial incluyen:

- **Estados Unidos:** Con empresas como Google, OpenAI y Microsoft, EE.UU. ha liderado el desarrollo de modelos de IA avanzados y su implementación en sectores clave como la salud, la tecnología y la defensa.

- **China:** Con un fuerte respaldo gubernamental, China ha avanzado en la IA con aplicaciones en vigilancia, comercio electrónico y transporte autónomo, además de contar con empresas como Baidu, Tencent y Alibaba.

- **Europa:** La Unión Europea ha centrado su enfoque en el desarrollo ético y regulado de la IA, con iniciativas para garantizar el uso responsable de estas tecnologías.

- **Japón y Corea del Sur:** Han utilizado la IA en la robótica, la manufactura y la asistencia a la población envejecida.

- **India y América Latina:** Países como India, Brasil y México han adoptado la IA en sectores como la educación, la banca y el comercio.

## Expansión en empresas y gobiernos

Muchas empresas han incorporado IA para mejorar la productividad y la eficiencia. Desde asistentes virtuales hasta análisis de datos en tiempo real, la IA ha revolucionado la manera en que operan las organizaciones. Los gobiernos, por su parte, han implementado sistemas de IA en seguridad ciudadana, gestión de recursos y atención médica.

## Crecimiento del número de usuarios de herramientas de IA

El uso de la IA ha crecido exponencialmente. Herramientas como ChatGPT han alcanzado millones de usuarios en pocos meses. Se estima que para 2025, más del 70% de las empresas utilizarán IA de alguna forma, y la adopción en el público general seguirá en aumento.

Este crecimiento global demuestra que la IA es una de las tecnologías más influyentes del siglo XXI, con un impacto cada vez mayor en la economía, la ciencia y la vida cotidiana.

# 3

# Importancia de la IA en la vida cotidiana y profesional

La inteligencia artificial ha pasado de ser un concepto de ciencia ficción a una herramienta presente en nuestro día a día. Aunque muchas personas aún no son plenamente conscientes de su impacto, la IA ya está mejorando la manera en que trabajamos, aprendemos, compramos, nos entretenemos y hasta cómo cuidamos nuestra salud.

En este capítulo, exploraremos de manera sencilla cómo la IA influye en nuestra vida cotidiana y profesional, con ejemplos prácticos y aplicaciones reales.

## 1. IA en la vida cotidiana

Si bien puede parecer que la inteligencia artificial es una tecnología reservada para expertos o grandes empresas, la realidad es que ya la usamos sin darnos cuenta. Cada vez que abrimos una aplicación en nuestro teléfono, realizamos una búsqueda en internet o interactuamos con dispositivos inteligentes, estamos aprovechando la IA.

## 1.1 Asistentes virtuales y dispositivos inteligentes

Los asistentes virtuales como Siri, Alexa y Google Assistant han cambiado la forma en que interactuamos con la tecnología. Con solo usar la voz, podemos:

- Pedir información del clima, noticias o datos de interés.

- Configurar recordatorios y alarmas.

- Reproducir música o podcasts.

- Controlar dispositivos inteligentes en el hogar (luces, termostatos, cámaras de seguridad).

Esto hace que la vida diaria sea más cómoda y eficiente, evitando la necesidad de escribir o realizar múltiples pasos para ejecutar una tarea.

## 1.2 Recomendaciones personalizadas

Cada vez que usamos Netflix, YouTube, Spotify o incluso plataformas de compras como Amazon, estamos interactuando con sistemas de IA que analizan nuestros hábitos y nos recomiendan contenido o productos que podrían interesarnos.

Por ejemplo, si sueles ver películas de ciencia ficción en Netflix, el algoritmo detectará tu preferencia y sugerirá más contenido similar. De la misma forma, si compras artículos deportivos en Amazon, la plataforma te mostrará productos relacionados.

## 1.3 IA en la salud y el bienestar

Las aplicaciones de salud como Fitbit, Apple Health y MyFitnessPal utilizan IA para monitorear nuestra actividad física, medir la calidad del sueño y darnos consejos personalizados. También existen dispositivos médicos que emplean IA para detectar signos tempranos de enfermedades, ayudando a los médicos a tomar decisiones más precisas.

## 1.4 Seguridad y autenticación

El reconocimiento facial y la autenticación por huella dactilar, utilizados en dispositivos móviles y sistemas de seguridad, son ejemplos claros del uso de IA en la protección de nuestros datos.

## 2. IA en el mundo profesional

La inteligencia artificial también está transformando la forma en que trabajamos. No importa si eres emprendedor, estudiante o trabajas en una gran empresa, la IA puede ayudarte a mejorar la productividad y la eficiencia.

## 2.1 IA en la educación

Plataformas como Duolingo, Coursera y Khan Academy utilizan IA para adaptar el aprendizaje a cada estudiante, ofreciendo cursos personalizados según el progreso y el nivel de dificultad adecuado.

Por ejemplo, si un estudiante aprende inglés en Duolingo y comete errores en ciertas estructuras gramaticales, la IA detectará estos patrones y ofrecerá más ejercicios específicos para reforzar esos aspectos.

## 2.2 IA en los negocios

Las empresas utilizan IA para analizar grandes volúmenes de datos y tomar mejores decisiones. Algunas aplicaciones incluyen:

- **Atención al cliente:** Chatbots como los de WhatsApp o Facebook Messenger automatizan respuestas y mejoran la comunicación con los clientes.

- **Marketing digital:** Algoritmos de IA analizan las interacciones en redes sociales y ayudan a personalizar campañas publicitarias.

- **Gestión financiera:** Bancos y empresas financieras emplean IA para detectar fraudes y mejorar la seguridad de las transacciones.

## 2.3 IA en la industria y la manufactura

La automatización mediante inteligencia artificial ha optimizado la producción en fábricas y almacenes. Robots inteligentes pueden ensamblar productos, detectar fallos en las líneas de producción y reducir costos operativos.

Un ejemplo claro es Tesla, que emplea IA para mejorar la producción de sus automóviles eléctricos, asegurando precisión y eficiencia en cada etapa del ensamblaje.

## 2.4 IA en el sector salud

En hospitales y clínicas, la IA ayuda a los médicos a diagnosticar enfermedades con mayor precisión. Por ejemplo, sistemas como IBM Watson analizan miles de estudios médicos en segundos para sugerir tratamientos adecuados para pacientes con cáncer.

Además, dispositivos como relojes inteligentes pueden detectar cambios en la frecuencia cardíaca y alertar sobre posibles problemas antes de que sean graves.

# 3. Beneficios de la IA en la vida cotidiana y profesional

Los principales beneficios de la inteligencia artificial incluyen:

- **Mayor eficiencia:** Automatiza tareas repetitivas, permitiendo que las personas se concentren en actividades más creativas y estratégicas.

- **Ahorro de tiempo:** Asistentes virtuales y herramientas inteligentes reducen el tiempo necesario para realizar tareas diarias.

- **Mejor toma de decisiones:** Empresas y profesionales pueden analizar datos con mayor precisión y hacer predicciones más acertadas.

- **Personalización:** Experiencias adaptadas a cada usuario, ya sea en entretenimiento, aprendizaje o consumo de productos.

- **Accesibilidad:** Permite a personas con discapacidades utilizar herramientas de reconocimiento de voz, traducción automática y más.

# 4

# Principales herramientas de IA en el mercado

La inteligencia artificial se ha diversificado en múltiples herramientas que facilitan la vida y el trabajo en diversas áreas. En este capítulo, exploraremos algunas de las herramientas más populares y cómo pueden ser utilizadas de manera efectiva.

## Herramientas de IA para generación de texto

1. **ChatGPT (OpenAI)**: Especializado en procesamiento de lenguaje natural, útil para generar texto, responder preguntas y asistir en tareas creativas.

2. **Jasper AI**: Plataforma avanzada para copywriting y marketing de contenidos con IA.

3. **Copy.ai**: Herramienta para redactar textos publicitarios y contenido de marketing de manera rápida.

4. **Writesonic**: Ideal para generar artículos, descripciones de productos y contenido SEO.

5. **Sudowrite**: Diseñada para escritores, ayuda a mejorar el estilo y la creatividad en la escritura.

6. **Rytr**: Alternativa económica para generar contenido en distintos tonos y estilos.

## Herramientas de IA para generación de imágenes

1. **DALL·E (OpenAI)**: Crea imágenes a partir de descripciones de texto con resultados sorprendentes.

2. **MidJourney**: Especializado en arte digital y diseño gráfico con estilos personalizados.

3. **Stable Diffusion**: IA de código abierto que permite generar imágenes con alto nivel de personalización.

4. **Deep Dream (Google)**: Transforma imágenes en obras artísticas surrealistas.

5. **Runway ML**: Plataforma para generar imágenes y editar videos con IA.

6. **Dream by Wombo**: Aplicación para crear arte digital basado en IA.

# Herramientas de IA para análisis de datos

1. **Google AutoML**: Permite a empresas y usuarios entrenar modelos de IA sin necesidad de conocimientos avanzados en programación.

2. **Tableau con IA**: Facilita la visualización de datos y análisis predictivos para negocios.

3. **Microsoft Azure Machine Learning**: Plataforma avanzada para el desarrollo y entrenamiento de modelos de IA.

4. **IBM Watson Analytics**: Herramienta de análisis de datos con IA integrada.

5. **DataRobot**: Automatiza el proceso de aprendizaje automático para análisis predictivos.

6. **H2O.ai**: Plataforma de aprendizaje automático con código abierto para análisis de datos avanzado.

# Herramientas de IA para automatización

1. **Zapier con IA**: Conecta aplicaciones y automatiza flujos de trabajo sin necesidad de código.

2. **UiPath**: Especializado en automatización robótica de procesos (RPA) para empresas.

3. **Microsoft Power Automate**: Permite la integración de herramientas y automatización de tareas repetitivas.

4. **IFTTT**: Plataforma que permite conectar aplicaciones y dispositivos para automatización personalizada.

5. **Make (anteriormente Integromat)**: Herramienta avanzada para crear flujos de trabajo automatizados.

6. **Automation Anywhere**: Plataforma robusta de automatización empresarial con IA.

## Herramientas de IA para desarrollo de software

1. **GitHub Copilot**: Asistente de codificación basado en IA que ayuda a programadores a escribir código más rápido.

2. **Tabnine**: IA que sugiere código en tiempo real dentro del entorno de desarrollo.

3. **Codex (OpenAI)**: Modelo de IA que traduce lenguaje natural en código de programación.

4. **Replit Ghostwriter**: Asistente para desarrollo colaborativo con funciones de IA.

5. **DeepCode**: Análisis de código con IA para detectar errores y mejorar calidad.

6. **CodeT5**: Modelo de IA especializado en generación de código y sugerencias en tiempo real.

Estas herramientas representan solo una parte del ecosistema de la inteligencia artificial en el mercado actual. A medida que la tecnología avanza, surgen nuevas aplicaciones que optimizan la productividad y mejoran la experiencia del usuario en múltiples ámbitos.

# 5

# IA para principiantes: Conceptos básicos

## Introducción

En este capítulo, exploraremos los conceptos fundamentales de la inteligencia artificial (IA) para que cualquier persona, sin importar su nivel de conocimiento, pueda comprender cómo funciona y cómo aplicarla en su vida diaria y profesional.

A medida que la IA avanza, su uso se vuelve cada vez más accesible. Ya no es necesario ser un experto en programación o en matemáticas avanzadas para aprovechar sus beneficios. Hoy en día, muchas herramientas de IA están diseñadas para ser intuitivas y fáciles de usar, permitiendo a cualquier persona mejorar su productividad, creatividad y eficiencia en diversas áreas.

El secreto para utilizar la IA de manera efectiva es conocer las herramientas adecuadas para cada tarea. Dependiendo de lo que quieras lograr, puedes utilizar asistentes de texto, generadores de imágenes, analizadores de datos y muchas otras aplicaciones impulsadas por inteligencia artificial. En este capítulo, aprenderás cómo empezar a usar la IA y qué herramientas específicas puedes emplear para diferentes necesidades.

## Ejemplos prácticos de uso de IA para principiantes

A continuación, presentamos algunos ejemplos concretos donde la IA puede ser útil, junto con comandos específicos para sacar el máximo provecho.

### *Ejemplo 1: Redacción de correos electrónicos (Herramienta recomendada: ChatGPT, Jasper AI)*

Si necesitas escribir correos formales o responder mensajes rápidamente, las herramientas de IA pueden ayudarte.

**Comando 1:** "Escribe un correo formal solicitando una reunión para discutir un nuevo proyecto."

**Comando 2:** "Genera una respuesta cortés a un cliente que solicita información sobre nuestros servicios."

### *Ejemplo 2: Creación de un plan de estudios personalizado (Herramienta recomendada: ChatGPT, Notion AI)*

La IA puede ayudarte a estructurar un plan de aprendizaje eficiente basado en tus objetivos y disponibilidad de tiempo.

**Comando 1:** "Crea un plan de estudios para aprender programación en Python en tres meses, dedicando 5 horas a la semana."

**Comando 2:** "Sugiere recursos gratuitos para aprender diseño gráfico desde cero."

## Ejemplo 3: Generación de ideas para redes sociales (Herramienta recomendada: Copy.ai, Writesonic)

Si eres creador de contenido, puedes aprovechar la IA para generar ideas y mejorar tus publicaciones.

**Comando 1:** "Dame 5 ideas creativas para publicaciones en Instagram sobre estilo de vida saludable."

**Comando 2:** "Escribe un tweet atractivo para promocionar un nuevo curso de marketing digital."

## Ejemplo 4: Planificación de comidas saludables (Herramienta recomendada: ChatGPT, Meal Planner AI)

Para quienes desean mejorar su alimentación, la IA puede sugerir menús personalizados.

**Comando 1:** "Genera un plan de comidas saludables para una semana con recetas fáciles y económicas."

**Comando 2:** "Sugiere opciones de almuerzo alto en proteínas y bajo en carbohidratos."

## *Ejemplo 5: Optimización del tiempo con IA (Herramienta recomendada: Reclaim AI, Motion)*

Las herramientas de IA pueden ayudarte a mejorar la organización de tu día a día.

**Comando 1:** "Crea una lista de tareas priorizadas para mejorar la productividad en el trabajo."

**Comando 2:** "Sugiere una rutina diaria para equilibrar trabajo, ejercicio y tiempo libre."

## *Ejemplo 6: Creación de presentaciones profesionales (Herramienta recomendada: Beautiful.ai, Tome AI)*

Si necesitas una presentación atractiva para el trabajo o estudios, la IA puede ayudarte con el diseño y contenido.

**Comando 1:** "Genera una estructura de presentación sobre tendencias en inteligencia artificial en 2025."

**Comando 2:** "Sugiere diapositivas clave para una presentación sobre liderazgo empresarial."

## *Ejemplo 7: Traducción y mejora de textos (Herramienta recomendada: DeepL, Grammarly, ChatGPT)*

Las herramientas de IA pueden traducir o mejorar textos en diferentes idiomas.

**Comando 1:** "Traduce este párrafo del español al inglés con un tono formal."

**Comando 2:** "Reescribe este texto para que suene más profesional y persuasivo."

## *Ejemplo 8: Generación de código para principiantes en programación (Herramienta recomendada: GitHub Copilot, ChatGPT, Codeium)*

La IA puede facilitar el aprendizaje de la programación generando fragmentos de código.

**Comando 1:** "Escribe un código en Python para calcular el área de un triángulo."

**Comando 2:** "Explica cómo funciona este código y sugiere mejoras: [pegar código aquí]."

Con estos ejemplos prácticos y comandos específicos, los principiantes pueden empezar a usar la IA de manera efectiva en su vida cotidiana y profesional. A continuación, exploraremos cómo los chatbots y asistentes virtuales pueden ser herramientas clave en diversas tareas.

# 6

# Chatbots y asistentes virtuales: Cómo sacarles provecho

Los chatbots y asistentes virtuales han revolucionado la forma en que interactuamos con la tecnología. Estos programas basados en inteligencia artificial permiten automatizar tareas, resolver dudas y mejorar la productividad en diversos ámbitos, desde la atención al cliente hasta la organización personal.

## ¿Qué son los chatbots y asistentes virtuales?

Los chatbots son programas diseñados para interactuar con los usuarios mediante texto o voz, respondiendo preguntas, proporcionando información o ejecutando tareas específicas. Pueden estar integrados en páginas web, aplicaciones de mensajería o sistemas empresariales.

Los asistentes virtuales, como Alexa, Siri y Google Assistant, son una versión más avanzada de los chatbots, ya que pueden gestionar tareas complejas mediante comandos de voz y aprendizaje automático, adaptándose a las preferencias del usuario con el tiempo.

## Tipos de chatbots y asistentes virtuales

Existen diferentes tipos de chatbots y asistentes virtuales, cada uno con funciones específicas:

1. **Chatbots de atención al cliente:** Utilizados en empresas para responder preguntas frecuentes, gestionar pedidos y resolver problemas.

2. **Asistentes personales:** Diseñados para ayudar en la organización diaria, como programar reuniones, establecer recordatorios y buscar información rápidamente.

3. **Chatbots de soporte técnico:** Ayudan a los usuarios a solucionar problemas técnicos sin necesidad de un agente humano.

4. **Asistentes de voz:** Programas como Alexa y Google Assistant que pueden controlar dispositivos domésticos inteligentes y responder a comandos de voz.

# Cómo sacar el máximo provecho de los chatbots y asistentes virtuales

Para optimizar el uso de estas herramientas, es importante conocer sus funciones y configurar adecuadamente sus opciones. Aquí hay algunos consejos:

- **Personalizar los comandos:** Configurar respuestas específicas según tus necesidades mejora la experiencia de uso.

- **Integrarlos con otras aplicaciones:** Sincronizar un asistente virtual con calendarios, correos y herramientas de trabajo automatiza tareas diarias.

- **Aprovechar las rutinas y automatizaciones:** Muchos asistentes permiten configurar secuencias de comandos para realizar varias acciones con una sola orden.

# Ejemplos prácticos de uso de chatbots y asistentes virtuales

## *1. Atención al cliente con chatbots (Herramienta recomendada: ChatGPT, Zendesk AI)*

**Ejemplo:** Una tienda en línea configura un chatbot para responder preguntas frecuentes sobre envíos y devoluciones.

- **Comando 1:** "Crea un chatbot que responda preguntas sobre los tiempos de envío y devolución de productos."

- **Comando 2:** "Programa un mensaje automático que informe a los clientes sobre promociones especiales."

## 2. Organización personal con asistentes virtuales (Herramienta recomendada: Google Assistant, Siri, Alexa)

**Ejemplo:** Un profesional utiliza un asistente virtual para gestionar su agenda y recordatorios.

- **Comando 1:** "Agrega una reunión con el equipo el lunes a las 10 a. m. en mi calendario."

- **Comando 2:** "Recuérdame comprar flores para el aniversario el viernes a las 6 p. m."

## 3. Soporte técnico automatizado (Herramienta recomendada: IBM Watson Assistant, Drift AI)

**Ejemplo:** Una empresa implementa un chatbot que ayuda a los empleados a solucionar problemas técnicos.

- **Comando 1:** "Configura un chatbot que guíe a los empleados en la recuperación de contraseñas."

- **Comando 2:** "Programa un bot que detecte y notifique problemas comunes en los sistemas de la empresa."

## 4. Control del hogar inteligente (Herramienta recomendada: Alexa, Google Home)

**Ejemplo:** Un usuario conecta su asistente de voz con dispositivos inteligentes para gestionar su hogar.

- **Comando 1:** "Enciende las luces del salón a las 7 p. m. todos los días."

- **Comando 2:** "Ajusta la temperatura del aire acondicionado a 22 grados antes de dormir."

Estos ejemplos muestran cómo los chatbots y asistentes virtuales pueden hacer la vida más fácil, desde mejorar la productividad hasta simplificar tareas cotidianas. Con una configuración adecuada y comandos personalizados, se pueden aprovechar al máximo estas tecnologías.

# 7

# Generación de contenido con IA: Textos, imágenes y videos

La inteligencia artificial ha revolucionado la manera en que se crea contenido digital. Desde la generación automática de textos hasta la creación de imágenes y videos realistas, las herramientas de IA han democratizado el acceso a la creatividad y han reducido significativamente el tiempo necesario para producir material de calidad. Tanto profesionales como principiantes pueden beneficiarse del uso de estas tecnologías para optimizar su flujo de trabajo y mejorar su eficiencia.

Antes, la producción de contenido de calidad requería habilidades especializadas y años de experiencia en redacción, diseño gráfico o edición de video. Hoy en día, con el auge de modelos avanzados de IA, cualquier persona puede generar textos atractivos, imágenes impresionantes y videos dinámicos en cuestión de minutos. Esta accesibilidad ha transformado industrias enteras, desde el marketing digital hasta el entretenimiento.

Uno de los factores más interesantes de la IA en la generación de contenido es su capacidad para adaptarse a diferentes estilos y necesidades. Un usuario puede solicitar un artículo con un tono formal o informal, pedir ilustraciones en un estilo específico o incluso generar videos con guiones personalizados. La clave para obtener los mejores resultados radica en saber cómo formular las instrucciones correctas, lo que se conoce como "prompting".

Además, la IA no solo facilita la creación de contenido, sino que también mejora la personalización. Las empresas pueden utilizar estas herramientas para producir materiales dirigidos a audiencias específicas, optimizando el impacto de su mensaje. En el ámbito educativo, los estudiantes y profesores pueden generar resúmenes, presentaciones y materiales de estudio en segundos. Las aplicaciones son prácticamente ilimitadas.

En este capítulo, exploraremos algunas de las herramientas más populares de IA para la generación de contenido, veremos cómo se utilizan y ofreceremos ejemplos prácticos para que puedas sacarles el máximo provecho. También analizaremos sus limitaciones y cómo combinarlas con la creatividad humana para lograr resultados óptimos. La inteligencia artificial no reemplaza el talento, pero puede potenciarlo de formas sorprendentes.

## Herramientas de IA para la generación de contenido

A continuación, presentamos algunas de las herramientas más utilizadas para la generación de textos, imágenes y videos con IA:

# 1. Generación de textos con IA

Las herramientas de IA para generación de textos permiten crear artículos, descripciones de productos, correos electrónicos y más en segundos. Algunas de las más destacadas incluyen:

- **ChatGPT (OpenAI):** Ideal para generar artículos, responder preguntas y redactar contenido variado.

- **Jasper AI:** Especializado en marketing y redacción publicitaria.

- **Copy.ai:** Diseñado para crear contenido publicitario y descripciones de productos.

- **Writesonic:** Permite generar textos para blogs, anuncios y redes sociales.

- **Rytr:** Ofrece opciones de redacción asistida con distintos estilos y tonos.

-

## *Ejemplo práctico:*

**Situación:** Un emprendedor necesita una descripción atractiva para su nuevo producto.

**Prompt en ChatGPT:** "Genera una descripción persuasiva para un smartwatch resistente al agua con monitor de ritmo cardíaco y GPS, dirigido a atletas."

**Respuesta generada:** "Descubre el smartwatch definitivo para atletas. Con resistencia al agua, GPS integrado y un avanzado monitor de ritmo cardíaco, este dispositivo es el compañero perfecto para cualquier entrenamiento. Mejora tu rendimiento con tecnología de punta y lleva tu actividad física al siguiente nivel."

## 2. Generación de imágenes con IA

Las herramientas de IA pueden crear imágenes realistas o artísticas a partir de descripciones textuales. Algunas de las más populares son:

- **DALL·E (OpenAI):** Genera imágenes a partir de texto con alta calidad.

- **MidJourney:** Enfocado en arte digital con un estilo único.

- **Stable Diffusion:** Permite la generación de imágenes de código abierto.

- **Deep Dream (Google):** Crea imágenes con un estilo artístico abstracto.

- **Runway ML:** Herramienta versátil para diseñadores y artistas.

### *Ejemplo práctico:*

**Situación:** Un diseñador necesita una imagen de un bosque futurista para un proyecto.

**Prompt en DALL·E:** "Un bosque futurista con árboles bioluminiscentes, caminos de cristal y un cielo estrellado con auroras."

**Imagen generada:** *(Se mostraría la imagen generada por la IA)*

## 3. Generación de videos con IA

Las plataformas de IA permiten crear videos automáticamente a partir de guiones o texto. Algunas herramientas útiles son:

- **Synthesia:** Crea videos con avatares animados y voces sintéticas.

- **Pictory:** Convierte texto en videos atractivos en minutos.

- **Runway ML:** También permite edición de video con IA avanzada.

- **DeepBrain AI:** Genera presentadores de noticias virtuales.

- **Rephrase.ai:** Personaliza videos con presentadores generados por IA.

### *Ejemplo práctico:*

**Situación:** Una empresa quiere crear un video promocional sin contratar actores.

**Prompt en Synthesia:** "Genera un video de 30 segundos con un presentador virtual explicando las ventajas de nuestro nuevo software de gestión empresarial."

**Video generado:** *(Se mostraría el video generado por la IA)*

La generación de contenido con IA ha abierto un mundo de posibilidades para creadores, empresas y usuarios en general. Estas herramientas permiten ahorrar tiempo, mejorar la calidad del contenido y democratizar la creatividad. Sin embargo, el verdadero potencial de la IA radica en su combinación con la creatividad humana. Saber cómo formular los prompts adecuados y revisar el contenido generado sigue siendo clave para obtener los mejores resultados.

# 8

# Análisis de datos con IA: Uso empresarial y personal

Vivimos en una era dominada por los datos. Desde los clics que realizamos en una web hasta los registros médicos o financieros, todo puede convertirse en información útil si se sabe interpretar. Aquí es donde entra la inteligencia artificial. La IA ha revolucionado el análisis de datos al permitir procesar volúmenes enormes de información en poco tiempo y obtener insights valiosos, tanto a nivel empresarial como personal.

Antes, interpretar datos complejos requería horas de trabajo humano y un conocimiento avanzado de estadística. Hoy, herramientas impulsadas por IA permiten a cualquier persona, incluso sin experiencia técnica, analizar patrones, identificar tendencias y tomar decisiones informadas con rapidez.

Este capítulo está diseñado para explicar cómo la inteligencia artificial facilita el análisis de datos, qué herramientas están disponibles y cómo aplicarlas en diferentes contextos. Ya sea que trabajes en una gran empresa, manejes un negocio pequeño o simplemente quieras optimizar tus finanzas personales, aquí aprenderás cómo hacerlo.

## ¿Qué es el análisis de datos con IA?

El análisis de datos con IA consiste en el uso de algoritmos y modelos automatizados para examinar grandes cantidades de información, detectar patrones y extraer conclusiones útiles. A diferencia del análisis tradicional, que es manual y lento, la IA puede detectar correlaciones invisibles al ojo humano y predecir comportamientos futuros con un alto nivel de precisión.

Los sistemas de IA que se usan para análisis de datos pueden estar basados en:

- **Aprendizaje automático (machine learning)**: Aprende de los datos pasados para predecir comportamientos futuros.

- **Procesamiento del lenguaje natural (NLP)**: Extrae información de textos no estructurados, como correos, reseñas o redes sociales.

- **Redes neuronales y deep learning**: Utilizadas para análisis más complejos como imágenes, voz o grandes volúmenes de datos estructurados.

# Herramientas populares de análisis de datos con IA

A continuación, te presentamos algunas de las herramientas más accesibles y poderosas para aplicar análisis de datos con inteligencia artificial:

## 1. Google AutoML

Permite entrenar modelos de machine learning sin necesidad de escribir código. Solo necesitas cargar tus datos y la plataforma se encarga del resto. Ideal para empresas pequeñas que quieren implementar IA sin contratar un equipo técnico.

**Usos comunes:**

- Predecir ventas.

- Clasificar correos o comentarios.

- Analizar imágenes para identificar productos o defectos.

## 2. Microsoft Azure Machine Learning

Una plataforma robusta y escalable que permite desarrollar, entrenar y desplegar modelos de machine learning. Es adecuada para empresas grandes que buscan automatizar procesos complejos.

**Usos comunes:**

- Detectar fraudes.

- Analizar la satisfacción del cliente.

- Predecir la demanda del mercado.

## 3. Tableau con IA (Tableau GPT)

Tableau es una de las herramientas de visualización de datos más usadas en el mundo. Su integración con inteligencia artificial permite a los usuarios obtener análisis automáticos, generar resúmenes e identificar anomalías sin conocimientos técnicos.

**Usos comunes:**

- Crear dashboards interactivos.

- Analizar datos financieros.

- Detectar comportamientos fuera de lo común.

## 4. Power BI + Copilot de Microsoft

Power BI permite crear informes visuales avanzados. Con la integración de Copilot, se pueden hacer preguntas en lenguaje natural y obtener respuestas automáticas basadas en los datos cargados.

**Usos comunes:**

- Informes de ventas.

- Seguimiento de métricas de negocio.

- Análisis de rendimiento en tiempo real.

## 5. MonkeyLearn

Especializada en análisis de texto. Ideal para extraer opiniones de reseñas, clasificar correos electrónicos o entender los comentarios en redes sociales.

**Usos comunes:**

- Análisis de sentimiento.

- Clasificación automática de tickets.

- Extracción de palabras clave en grandes volúmenes de texto.

## 6. Qlik Sense con IA

Qlik Sense es una plataforma de inteligencia empresarial que, con la ayuda de IA, guía a los usuarios para descubrir patrones y tendencias en los datos mediante recomendaciones automáticas y visualizaciones interactivas.

**Usos comunes:**

- Análisis de datos de clientes.

- Optimización de procesos logísticos.

- Análisis de inventarios.

# Aplicaciones prácticas del análisis de datos con IA

### *Ejemplo 1: Mejora de campañas de marketing digital*

**IA recomendada:** Tableau + IA o Google AutoML

Una empresa que invierte en anuncios digitales puede usar IA para analizar qué tipo de publicaciones generan más clics, qué horarios son más efectivos y qué perfiles de usuario convierten más. Con estos datos, se optimizan las campañas futuras.

### Comandos prácticos:

- "Analiza las métricas de conversión de las últimas 4 campañas."

- "Identifica qué tipo de contenido tuvo mejor rendimiento en Facebook."

### *Ejemplo 2: Predicción de ventas en un eCommerce*

**IA recomendada:** Azure Machine Learning o Power BI + Copilot

Con la IA se pueden predecir ventas futuras basadas en el comportamiento histórico, eventos especiales y tendencias de mercado.

## Comandos prácticos:

- "Predice las ventas de diciembre con base en los últimos tres años."

- "Compara el comportamiento de compra en Black Friday y Navidad."

## *Ejemplo 3: Análisis de satisfacción del cliente*

**IA recomendada:** MonkeyLearn

Recogiendo opiniones de los clientes en redes, reseñas y encuestas, una empresa puede clasificar los comentarios por sentimiento y detectar áreas de mejora.

## Comandos prácticos:

- "Clasifica estas reseñas por positivas, negativas y neutras."

- "Extrae los temas más mencionados en comentarios negativos."

## *Ejemplo 4: Gestión financiera personal*

**IA recomendada:** Power BI o Tableau con IA

Un usuario puede conectar sus gastos mensuales y la IA le sugiere cómo ahorrar, en qué gasta más y cómo ajustar su presupuesto.

**Comandos prácticos:**

- "Muestra un gráfico de mis gastos mensuales por categoría."

- "Sugiere formas de reducir gastos basados en los últimos tres meses."

## Recomendaciones para empezar

- **Empieza con tus propios datos.** Usa tus finanzas personales, datos de redes o información de tu negocio.

- **No necesitas programar.** Muchas herramientas ofrecen interfaces visuales y comandos en lenguaje natural.

- **Compara resultados.** Asegúrate de que los patrones detectados por la IA tienen sentido antes de tomar decisiones.

- **Haz pruebas pequeñas.** Antes de aplicar IA a gran escala, experimenta con proyectos pequeños.

El análisis de datos con IA está al alcance de todos. Solo necesitas una herramienta adecuada y una pregunta clara que responder. Cuanto más específicos sean tus objetivos, más útiles serán los resultados que obtengas.

# 9

# Automatización con IA: Tareas diarias y profesionales

La automatización mediante inteligencia artificial se ha convertido en una herramienta clave para optimizar tareas tanto en el ámbito personal como profesional. Gracias al avance de la IA, ahora es posible delegar procesos repetitivos, mejorar la gestión del tiempo y aumentar la eficiencia sin necesidad de conocimientos técnicos avanzados. En este capítulo vamos a explorar cómo la automatización puede cambiar tu día a día, qué herramientas utilizar y cómo configurarlas para obtener el máximo beneficio.

## ¿Por qué automatizar con IA?

Automatizar tareas con IA tiene múltiples ventajas:

- **Ahorro de tiempo:** Las tareas rutinarias se ejecutan solas, lo que libera tiempo para actividades más importantes.

- **Reducción de errores:** Al automatizar, se eliminan muchos errores humanos derivados de la repetición o la fatiga.

- **Mayor productividad:** Puedes hacer más cosas en menos tiempo y con mejor calidad.

- **Toma de decisiones basada en datos:** Muchas herramientas automatizadas también analizan datos y te dan recomendaciones inteligentes.

## Tipos de tareas que se pueden automatizar

La IA permite automatizar tareas como:

- Envío de correos electrónicos.

- Programación de publicaciones en redes sociales.

- Gestión de agenda y reuniones.

- Seguimiento de ventas y CRM.

- Clasificación y respuesta automática de correos.

- Generación de reportes periódicos.

- Procesamiento de documentos y formularios.

- Traducción y corrección de textos.

## Herramientas de automatización basadas en IA

A continuación, presentamos algunas de las herramientas más accesibles y potentes para automatización inteligente:

# 1. Zapier con OpenAI

Zapier permite conectar aplicaciones entre sí para que trabajen de forma automática. Combinado con OpenAI, puedes automatizar flujos complejos con inteligencia conversacional.

*Ejemplo práctico:* Automatizar la respuesta a formularios de clientes.

- **Prompt para OpenAI:**" Resume las respuestas del formulario y genera una respuesta amable para el cliente."

- **Flujo en Zapier:** Google Forms → OpenAI → Gmail

# 2. Make (antes Integromat)

Make permite crear flujos automatizados más complejos, con filtros, ramas y análisis avanzado de datos.

**Ejemplo práctico:** Detectar menciones de tu marca en Twitter y generar un resumen diario.

- **Herramienta IA utilizada:** OpenAI o Claude

- **Flujo:** Twitter → OpenAI (resumen) → Email diario

# 3. Notion AI

Además de ser un espacio de trabajo colaborativo, Notion AI permite generar y organizar contenido automáticamente.

*Ejemplo práctico:* Organizar notas de reuniones y generar resúmenes automáticos.

- **Prompt sugerido:**" Resume esta nota en puntos clave, genera un plan de acción y detecta tareas pendientes."

- **Flujo:** Notas → IA → Base de tareas

# 4. ChatGPT + Plugins

ChatGPT con plugins como Zapier, Browsing o Wolfram puede funcionar como un asistente de automatización avanzado.

*Ejemplo práctico:* Preguntar a ChatGPT qué tareas tienes programadas y recibir recordatorios.

- **Prompt:**¿" Qué tengo pendiente esta semana? Avísame si olvido algo importante."

- **Requiere conexión con Google Calendar y tareas pendientes.**

# 5. Microsoft Power Automate

Plataforma de automatización empresarial integrada con Microsoft 365. Conecta Outlook, Excel, Teams y más.

*Ejemplo práctico:* Automatizar la entrada de datos en una hoja de cálculo desde correos recibidos.

- **Flujo:** Outlook → Power Automate → Excel

- **IA sugerida:** Microsoft AI Builder para análisis de contenido.

# 6. IFTTT (If This Then That)

Una de las herramientas más simples y accesibles. Permite conectar dispositivos, apps y servicios con condiciones lógicas básicas.

*Ejemplo práctico:* Si subes una foto a Instagram, que se guarde en tu Drive y se publique en Twitter.

- **Flujo:** Instagram → Google Drive → Twitter

- **IA sugerida (opcional):** Añadir descripción automática con GPT.

# 7. ElevenLabs + IA de texto a voz

Automatiza la creación de audios para entrenamiento, redes sociales o atención al cliente.

*Ejemplo práctico:* Cada vez que se publica un blog nuevo, generar un audio resumen con voz natural.

- **Flujo:** RSS → ChatGPT (resumen) → ElevenLabs (audio) → Email

- **Prompt:**" Resume este artículo y conviértelo en un guion atractivo para leer en voz alta."

## Automatización en la vida diaria

Incluso si no trabajas en una empresa, puedes beneficiarte de la automatización:

- **Tareas domésticas:** Recordatorios automáticos para limpieza, compras o citas médicas.

- **Finanzas personales:** Categorización de gastos, alertas de pagos próximos.

- **Correo personal:** Respuestas automáticas para ciertos remitentes.

- **Aprendizaje:** Recordatorios para estudiar, resúmenes de artículos, flashcards generadas automáticamente.

## Automatización en el entorno profesional

En empresas, la IA automatiza procesos como:

- Onboarding de empleados.

- Análisis y segmentación de clientes.

- Gestión documental.

- Atención al cliente con chatbots inteligentes.

- Generación de reportes y dashboards.

## Recomendaciones para empezar

1. **Empieza con una tarea simple** que realices de forma repetitiva.

2. **Identifica las herramientas que ya usas** (Gmail, Excel, Slack, etc.).

3. **Usa una plataforma sencilla** como Zapier o IFTTT para hacer tus primeros flujos.

4. **Integra una IA generativa** para respuestas, resúmenes o análisis automáticos.

5. **Evalúa y ajusta** el flujo con el tiempo para mejorar su eficacia.

La automatización con IA no solo ahorra tiempo, sino que transforma la forma en la que trabajamos y vivimos. No hace falta ser programador ni experto. Basta con conocer bien tus necesidades, aprender a usar una o dos herramientas, y dar el primer paso. Una vez que automatizas la primera tarea, verás que muchas más pueden seguir el mismo camino.

**¿Quieres empezar?** Piensa en una tarea que repitas a diario y que no requiera creatividad. Luego, elige una herramienta y prueba. El cambio puede ser más fácil de lo que crees.

# 10

# IA en el desarrollo de software y programación

La inteligencia artificial ha transformado el mundo del desarrollo de software. Donde antes los procesos eran manuales, repetitivos y consumían mucho tiempo, hoy las herramientas basadas en IA permiten escribir código, depurar errores, probar funcionalidades y optimizar el rendimiento de manera más eficiente.

## ¿Por qué usar IA en programación?

1. **Ahorro de tiempo:** Automatiza tareas repetitivas como completar código, generar documentación o revisar errores.

2. **Mejora la calidad del código:** Herramientas de IA ayudan a identificar errores y sugerir mejoras de forma proactiva.

3. **Aprendizaje asistido:** Los programadores novatos pueden aprender más rápido con asistentes que explican conceptos, sintaxis y estructuras.

4. **Colaboración:** Plataformas como GitHub Copilot facilitan el trabajo en equipo sugiriendo código compatible con el estilo del proyecto.

## Principales herramientas de IA para programación

1. **GitHub Copilot:** Asistente de codificación desarrollado por GitHub y OpenAI. Sugiere líneas completas de código y funciones mientras escribes.

2. **Amazon CodeWhisperer:** Proporciona recomendaciones de código, similar a Copilot, y se integra con AWS.

3. **Tabnine:** Autocompletado de código basado en IA, compatible con múltiples lenguajes y editores como VS Code.

4. **Kite:** Otro asistente que ofrece autocompletado inteligente para Python, JavaScript y otros lenguajes.

5. **Codex (OpenAI):** Motor detrás de Copilot, puede ejecutarse directamente desde entornos personalizados con API.

6. **Codeium:** Alternativa gratuita con soporte para más de 20 lenguajes de programación.

# Ejemplos prácticos de uso

## Ejemplo 1: Autocompletado de funciones

- Herramienta: GitHub Copilot

- Escenario: Estás escribiendo una función en Python para calcular la media de una lista de números.

- Comando:
  ```
  def calcular_media(lista):
  ```

  - Copilot automáticamente sugerirá el cuerpo de la función.

## Ejemplo 2: Generar código desde instrucciones en lenguaje natural

- Herramienta: OpenAI Codex

- Prompt: "Escribe una función en JavaScript que verifique si una palabra es palíndroma"

- Resultado: Generación automática del código con explicación línea por línea.

## Ejemplo 3: Asistente de depuración

- Herramienta: Tabnine + extensiones del IDE

- Escenario: El código lanza una excepción y necesitas encontrar el error.

- Tabnine sugiere correcciones o modificaciones que solucionan el problema.

### *Ejemplo 4: Documentación automática*

- Herramienta: Kite o Copilot

- Escribes una función compleja y la IA genera automáticamente los comentarios explicativos.

### *Ejemplo 5: Aprendizaje personalizado*

- Herramienta: ChatGPT

- Prompt: "Explícame cómo funcionan las clases en Python con ejemplos simples"

- Obtienes una explicación estructurada, con ejemplos listos para copiar y ejecutar.

## Cómo empezar

1. **Instala un editor compatible:** Visual Studio Code es el más común.

2. **Elige una extensión o plugin:** Por ejemplo, GitHub Copilot o Tabnine.

3. **Crea un archivo de código:** Abre un proyecto o inicia uno nuevo.

4. **Empieza a escribir:** Las herramientas de IA te sugerirán líneas, correcciones o mejoras.

5. **Aprovecha los prompts:** Si usas modelos como Codex o ChatGPT, formula instrucciones claras y específicas.

## Consejos para sacar el máximo partido

- **Sé claro:** Cuanto más específico sea el prompt o el nombre de tu función, mejores sugerencias tendrás.

- **Aprende del código generado:** No lo copies ciegamente, revisa y entiende cómo funciona.

- **Combina herramientas:** Usa ChatGPT para explicar y Copilot para codificar.

- **Personaliza tu entorno:** Configura tu IDE para integrar varias herramientas de IA y optimizar tu flujo de trabajo.

## Consideraciones éticas y límites

Aunque la IA puede ayudarte a ser más eficiente, no reemplaza el juicio de un programador humano. Asegúrate de:

- Revisar todo el código generado.

- No depender ciegamente de las sugerencias.

- Tener en cuenta temas de propiedad intelectual si usas código sugerido por IA.

La IA aplicada a la programación permite acelerar el desarrollo, reducir errores y fomentar el aprendizaje continuo. Con el uso inteligente de herramientas como Copilot, Codex, Tabnine o ChatGPT, tanto principiantes como expertos pueden mejorar su flujo de trabajo y crear soluciones más eficientes.

# 11

# Seguridad y ética en la Inteligencia Artificial

La inteligencia artificial ha crecido exponencialmente en capacidad y en alcance, y con ello surgen preocupaciones legítimas sobre su seguridad, su uso responsable y las implicaciones éticas que conlleva. A medida que más personas, empresas y gobiernos incorporan la IA en sus actividades diarias, resulta fundamental establecer principios y mecanismos que aseguren que estas tecnologías no causen daño, no perpetúen injusticias ni violen la privacidad o los derechos humanos.

## 1. ¿Por qué es importante hablar de ética en la IA?

La ética en la inteligencia artificial es esencial porque estas tecnologías no operan en el vacío. Son creadas, entrenadas y utilizadas por personas, y por tanto reflejan nuestras intenciones, sesgos y estructuras sociales. Un sistema de IA puede parecer imparcial, pero si ha sido entrenado con datos sesgados, replicará e incluso amplificará esas desigualdades.

Ejemplos ya han salido a la luz: algoritmos de contratación que discriminan por género, sistemas de reconocimiento facial menos precisos para personas de piel oscura, o aplicaciones que manipulan la información con fines políticos. Esto nos obliga a tomar conciencia sobre cómo se desarrollan estas herramientas y cómo se aplican en la práctica.

## 2. Principales riesgos de la IA mal gestionada

La IA puede representar varios tipos de riesgos si no se implementa con cuidado:

- **Privacidad y vigilancia:** Muchas aplicaciones de IA procesan grandes cantidades de datos personales. Un mal uso puede derivar en vigilancia masiva, pérdida de anonimato o exposición de datos sensibles.

- **Discriminación algorítmica:** Si el entrenamiento de una IA se basa en datos históricos con prejuicios, reproducirá esos prejuicios. Esto es crítico en áreas como justicia, seguros, préstamos o contratación.

- **Falta de transparencia:** Algunas decisiones automatizadas son difíciles de explicar (lo que se conoce como "caja negra"). Esto complica la auditoría o el entendimiento de por qué un sistema toma ciertas decisiones.

- **Dependencia excesiva:** El uso intensivo de sistemas de IA sin supervisión puede generar dependencia tecnológica, donde las personas confían ciegamente en decisiones automatizadas sin cuestionarlas.

- **Desinformación y manipulación:** Con tecnologías como los deepfakes o los generadores de texto, se puede difundir información falsa de manera masiva y muy realista, afectando la democracia y la opinión pública.

# 3. Marco legal y regulatorio

Dado el impacto de la IA, varios países y organizaciones internacionales están creando marcos legales y éticos. Algunos ejemplos:

- **Unión Europea:** Con su propuesta de la Ley de IA, la UE busca clasificar las aplicaciones según su riesgo y establecer reglas claras sobre transparencia, uso de datos, derechos del usuario y responsabilidad legal.

- **Estados Unidos:** Ha adoptado un enfoque más flexible, donde diferentes estados desarrollan sus propias leyes, aunque existen esfuerzos federales para establecer principios comunes.

- **ONU y UNESCO:** Han propuesto principios éticos universales que incluyen la equidad, la transparencia, la inclusión y la sostenibilidad.

# 4. Principios éticos fundamentales en la IA

A nivel internacional, se han consensuado varios principios éticos clave que deben guiar el desarrollo y uso de la inteligencia artificial:

- **Transparencia:** Los usuarios deben entender cómo funcionan los sistemas y por qué toman determinadas decisiones.

- **Justicia:** Evitar que la IA refuerce desigualdades. Esto implica detectar y corregir sesgos.

- **Responsabilidad:** Establecer claramente quién es responsable por los errores o daños causados por una IA.

- **Privacidad:** Proteger los datos personales usados en el entrenamiento o funcionamiento del sistema.

- **Seguridad:** Garantizar que los sistemas sean robustos y no vulnerables a fallos o ciberataques.

# 5. ¿Cómo pueden los usuarios protegerse y actuar con responsabilidad?

Aunque gran parte de la responsabilidad recae en los desarrolladores y las empresas, los usuarios también deben adoptar una actitud consciente y crítica frente al uso de estas tecnologías. Algunas recomendaciones:

- **Informarse sobre las herramientas que usan.** Saber qué datos recolectan, cómo toman decisiones y si han sido auditadas.

- **Leer las políticas de privacidad.** Muchas veces, aceptamos términos sin saber qué datos cedemos.

- **Evitar compartir información sensible.** Especialmente si la IA está en fase de prueba o no tiene garantías de protección de datos.

- **Cuestionar los resultados.** No asumir que todo lo que dice un chatbot o una herramienta de IA es correcto o imparcial.

- **Reportar fallos o usos indebidos.** Las plataformas suelen tener canales para denunciar abusos o errores.

# 6. El rol de las empresas tecnológicas

Las empresas que desarrollan IA tienen una enorme responsabilidad. No basta con crear productos eficientes, también deben asegurarse de que sean justos, seguros y auditables. Esto implica:

- Hacer pruebas exhaustivas para detectar sesgos.

- Incorporar diversidad en los equipos de desarrollo.

- Publicar documentación técnica clara.

- Establecer mecanismos de supervisión y control.

- Crear políticas de acceso responsable a sus tecnologías.

## 7. IA responsable: ejemplos positivos

Afortunadamente, también hay muchos ejemplos de uso responsable y ético de la IA:

- **IA para detectar noticias falsas.** Herramientas que ayudan a verificar fuentes y alertar sobre desinformación.

- **Asistentes virtuales accesibles.** Chatbots adaptados para personas con discapacidades visuales o auditivas.

- **Sistemas de salud con protección de datos.** Algoritmos que diagnostican enfermedades pero en entornos controlados, sin compartir datos sensibles.

- **Análisis de justicia predictiva revisado por humanos.** Modelos que ayudan a tomar decisiones judiciales pero con revisión y control humano obligatorio.

## 8. Hacia una cultura digital ética

El futuro de la IA no se define solo por el código o los algoritmos, sino por cómo decidimos usarla. Crear una cultura ética implica educar a las personas, desde los usuarios más básicos hasta los ingenieros que diseñan los modelos.

Es importante fomentar:

- El pensamiento crítico digital.

- La conciencia sobre sesgos y discriminación.

- La demanda de transparencia por parte de las plataformas.

- La participación en el debate público sobre qué tipo de tecnología queremos.

## 9. ¿Qué sigue? Retos y oportunidades

Los próximos años serán clave para establecer las bases de una inteligencia artificial responsable. Algunos de los retos pendientes son:

- Lograr una regulación global coherente.

- Aumentar la educación en ética digital.

- Hacer que los sistemas sean explicables y auditables.

- Equilibrar innovación con derechos humanos.

Pero también hay grandes oportunidades: la IA bien utilizada puede reducir desigualdades, mejorar la calidad de vida, hacer más eficiente la gestión pública y permitir avances científicos impensables hace solo una década.

# 12

# Mejorando la productividad con IA: Trucos y consejos

La inteligencia artificial puede ser una gran aliada para mejorar la productividad personal y profesional. Desde la automatización de tareas repetitivas hasta el apoyo en la toma de decisiones complejas, las herramientas basadas en IA permiten aprovechar mejor el tiempo y los recursos. Este capítulo te enseñará cómo usar la IA para trabajar de forma más inteligente, no más dura.

## ¿Por qué la IA mejora la productividad?

El objetivo de la IA es optimizar procesos. Esto significa hacer más en menos tiempo, reducir errores, anticipar necesidades y liberar a las personas para que se enfoquen en lo que realmente importa. Cuando usamos bien estas herramientas, se convierten en asistentes incansables que nos ayudan a organizar, ejecutar y mejorar nuestras actividades.

Además, la IA aprende y se adapta. Esto significa que cuanto más la uses, más precisa se vuelve en ayudarte. Aplicada a la productividad, esto puede traducirse en agendas mejor gestionadas, respuestas más rápidas, correos redactados automáticamente, ideas generadas con base en tu estilo o incluso presentaciones armadas desde cero.

## Herramientas clave para aumentar la productividad

Aquí algunas de las herramientas de IA más útiles cuando se trata de productividad:

- **ChatGPT / Claude / Gemini**: redactan correos, sintetizan información, ayudan con ideas, revisan textos, etc.

- **Notion AI**: organiza tareas, toma notas automáticas, genera resúmenes y crea estructuras para documentos.

- **Fireflies.ai / Otter.ai**: transcriben reuniones, detectan acciones clave y ayudan a hacer seguimientos.

- **Clockwise**: optimiza tu calendario para que tengas más bloques de tiempo libre y productivo.

- **Zapier + IA**: automatiza flujos entre apps, usando lógica impulsada por inteligencia artificial.

- **Krisp**: elimina ruidos de fondo en llamadas y genera resúmenes automáticos.

## Organización personal y gestión del tiempo

La IA puede ayudarte a organizarte mejor. Puedes usar asistentes virtuales para agendar reuniones automáticamente según disponibilidad, establecer recordatorios o incluso sugerir el mejor momento para trabajar en una tarea específica. Herramientas como Motion, Clockwise o Google Calendar (con funciones inteligentes activadas) pueden ayudarte a:

- Reorganizar tu calendario para que tengas bloques de trabajo profundo.

- Predecir cuánto tiempo te tomará una tarea.

- Sugerir reprogramaciones en función de prioridades.

*Ejemplo práctico*: Usando Notion AI puedes escribir:
**Prompt**: *"Crea una lista de tareas con prioridad alta, media y baja basada en estas actividades: revisar informes, enviar propuestas, responder correos, planear evento, hacer seguimiento a cliente, estudiar nuevo software."*
Y recibirás una estructura ordenada automáticamente.

## Automatización de tareas repetitivas

La IA puede identificar patrones en tus actividades diarias. Si siempre realizas ciertas acciones después de una reunión (por ejemplo, enviar un correo resumen o actualizar un CRM), puedes automatizar esos pasos. Herramientas como Zapier o

Make permiten combinar lógica condicional con inteligencia artificial para que esto suceda sin intervención humana.

*Ejemplo práctico:*
Automatizar con Zapier + ChatGPT:
**Trigger**: reunión en Zoom finaliza
**Acción**: enviar audio a Otter.ai para transcripción
**Acción siguiente**: resumen generado por ChatGPT
**Acción final**: resumen se envía automáticamente por email al equipo.

## Redacción, corrección y generación de contenido

Una de las formas más conocidas en que la IA mejora la productividad es a través de la redacción. Herramientas como Grammarly, ChatGPT o Jasper AI permiten redactar desde emails hasta propuestas complejas en segundos, o revisar textos para asegurar que estén bien escritos.

*Ejemplo práctico:*
**Prompt**: *"Escribe un email profesional para pedir una prórroga de entrega de un informe, manteniendo un tono formal pero empático."*

## Toma de decisiones y análisis de información

La IA puede ayudarte a tomar decisiones más informadas. Herramientas como Tableau con IA, Microsoft Copilot o Google Sheets con inteligencia artificial pueden detectar patrones en tus datos, generar predicciones o incluso explicarte tendencias que no habías notado.

*Ejemplo práctico:*
Subes un conjunto de datos de ventas a Google Sheets y usas el asistente con IA para preguntarle:
**Prompt**: *"¿Qué día de la semana tenemos más ventas? ¿Hay una tendencia en ciertos productos según el mes?"*

Recibes gráficos, explicaciones y sugerencias de acción.

## Optimización del aprendizaje y desarrollo personal

Las herramientas de IA también ayudan a aprender mejor. Plataformas como Khan Academy con IA, Duolingo, o incluso YouTube con transcripción automática y resumen, permiten personalizar el ritmo y el enfoque del aprendizaje.

*Ejemplo práctico:*
**Prompt**: *"Explícame los fundamentos de la economía conductual en un lenguaje sencillo con ejemplos cotidianos."*
Respuesta: contenido adaptado a tu nivel, con claridad y ejemplos accesibles.

## Consejos clave para mejorar tu productividad con IA

1.  **Empieza con una necesidad clara**: no uses IA por usarla. Identifica qué te está robando tiempo.

2. **Sé específico en tus prompts**: cuanto más claro seas, mejores resultados obtendrás.

3. **Integra IA en tus flujos diarios**: no necesitas cambiar todo. Empieza por una tarea.

4. **Evalúa y ajusta**: revisa si la herramienta realmente está ayudándote. Si no, modifica cómo la usas.

5. **Combina herramientas**: usa ChatGPT para redactar, Notion AI para estructurar y Zapier para automatizar, todo en una sola cadena de eficiencia.

La IA no reemplaza tu capacidad, la amplifica. Te permite hacer más, con menos esfuerzo, y enfocarte en lo que realmente importa. Al dominar su uso, puedes transformar tu manera de trabajar y vivir, recuperando tiempo y energía para las tareas que necesitan tu atención plena.

# 13

# Personalización y entrenamiento de modelos de IA

Uno de los mayores avances en la inteligencia artificial moderna es la posibilidad de personalizar y entrenar modelos según las necesidades específicas del usuario o de una organización. Esta capacidad permite adaptar la IA a contextos muy concretos, logrando resultados mucho más precisos y útiles.

## ¿Qué significa personalizar un modelo de IA?

Personalizar un modelo de IA consiste en modificar su comportamiento para que responda de forma adecuada a un dominio, sector o tipo de lenguaje concreto. Por ejemplo, una empresa puede entrenar un modelo para que responda como un asesor legal, un agente de atención al cliente, o incluso como un asistente de ventas que entiende los productos y procesos de la compañía.

# ¿Qué se necesita para personalizar un modelo?

- **Datos representativos**: Lo más importante es contar con ejemplos claros y suficientes. Cuanto más representativos y limpios sean los datos, mejor se entrenará el modelo.

- **Plataforma o entorno de entrenamiento**: OpenAI, Google Vertex AI, Amazon SageMaker y otras plataformas ofrecen herramientas para personalizar modelos de lenguaje y visión.

- **Recursos computacionales**: Aunque existen herramientas que permiten entrenamiento en la nube sin conocimientos técnicos avanzados, si se busca un nivel alto de personalización, se requieren GPUs y servidores con gran capacidad.

## Tipos de personalización

1. **Entrenamiento fino (fine-tuning)**: Se parte de un modelo ya entrenado (como GPT-3 o GPT-4) y se le entrena con un conjunto de datos nuevos para adaptar su comportamiento.

2. **Instrucciones personalizadas (custom instructions)**: Algunos modelos permiten establecer preferencias sin necesidad de reentrenar. Por ejemplo, ChatGPT permite especificar "cómo debe responder" el asistente.

3. **Bases de datos conectadas (RAG - Retrieval-Augmented Generation)**: Esta técnica combina un

modelo base con una base de conocimiento externa que consulta para dar respuestas más precisas.

## Herramientas para entrenar y personalizar modelos

- **OpenAI Fine-Tuning API**: Ideal para personalizar modelos de GPT usando tus propios ejemplos de conversación o documentos.

- **Hugging Face**: Permite crear, modificar y entrenar modelos en un entorno colaborativo con acceso a modelos preentrenados.

- **Google Vertex AI**: Plataforma empresarial para entrenamiento y despliegue de modelos personalizados.

- **Amazon SageMaker**: Ideal para usuarios técnicos que desean desarrollar modelos personalizados desde cero.

- **LlamaIndex + LangChain**: Muy útiles para construir aplicaciones que combinan IA con bases de datos propias o documentos.

## Ejemplos prácticos

*Ejemplo 1: Personalizar un chatbot para atención al cliente*

IA recomendada: GPT-4 (vía OpenAI) o Claude

Pasos:

1. Recopilar conversaciones reales de atención al cliente.

2. Limpiar los datos y estructurarlos en formato pregunta-respuesta.

3. Usar la API de Fine-Tuning de OpenAI para entrenar el modelo.

Prompt personalizado: "Eres un agente de atención al cliente de la empresa ACME. Responde siempre de forma profesional, clara y amigable."

## *Ejemplo 2: Entrenar un modelo para asesoramiento legal básico*

IA recomendada: GPT-4 o Google PaLM

Pasos:

1. Recopilar preguntas frecuentes y respuestas jurídicas revisadas por expertos.

2. Clasificar por temas (contratos, laboral, fiscal, etc.).

3. Entrenar el modelo para cada categoría o usar RAG para conectarlo a una base legal.

Prompt personalizado: "Actúa como un abogado especializado en derecho laboral. Responde con base en las leyes españolas actuales."

## Ejemplo 3: Adaptar un generador de contenido para una marca específica

IA recomendada: Jasper o ChatGPT con instrucciones personalizadas

Pasos:

1. Definir el tono de la marca (formal, cercano, técnico, etc.).

2. Entrenar al modelo con artículos, publicaciones y correos anteriores.

3. Ajustar el estilo de salida según el canal (blog, redes, emails).

Prompt personalizado: "Eres el generador de contenido de la marca de tecnología VerdeDigital. Escribe un post sobre sostenibilidad tecnológica en un tono inspirador, directo y con lenguaje sencillo."

## Ejemplo 4: Asistente educativo personalizado para un curso

IA recomendada: ChatGPT con datos embebidos o Google Bard

Pasos:

1. Crear un índice del curso con los contenidos principales.

2. Proveer ejemplos, definiciones y ejercicios resueltos.

3. Usar LangChain para conectar la IA con documentos y PDFs del curso.

Prompt personalizado: "Eres un asistente educativo del curso de Introducción a la Psicología. Responde a las preguntas del estudiante usando exclusivamente el contenido del curso proporcionado."

## Ventajas de personalizar modelos de IA

• Respuestas más precisas y relevantes

• Alineación con los valores o lenguaje de la marca

• Mejora en la eficiencia y automatización de procesos

• Reducción de errores o respuestas genéricas

## Consideraciones éticas y legales

Al personalizar modelos, especialmente cuando se utilizan datos sensibles o privados, es fundamental garantizar:

• El consentimiento para el uso de datos

• La anonimización de la información personal

• El cumplimiento de leyes como GDPR o la LOPD

## Recomendaciones finales

- Empieza con modelos ya existentes y ajusta poco a poco.

- Evalúa constantemente la calidad de las respuestas generadas.

- Combina personalización con técnicas como prompt engineering para mejores resultados.

- Documenta el proceso para facilitar ajustes futuros.

# 14

# Errores comunes y limitaciones de la IA

La inteligencia artificial ha transformado múltiples industrias y aspectos de la vida diaria. Sin embargo, su uso no está exento de problemas. Comprender los errores más comunes y las limitaciones inherentes a la tecnología es clave para aplicarla con responsabilidad y eficiencia. Este capítulo te servirá como advertencia, guía y punto de reflexión para que puedas sacarle el mayor partido a la IA sin caer en malas prácticas.

## Errores comunes al usar IA

## 1. Esperar resultados perfectos desde el principio

Uno de los errores más comunes entre quienes empiezan a usar IA es esperar que la herramienta proporcione soluciones exactas o mágicas desde el primer intento. La IA funciona mejor cuando se le entrena o se le da contexto suficiente. Esto aplica especialmente a los modelos de lenguaje como ChatGPT:

cuanto más específico y claro sea tu prompt, mejores serán los resultados.

*Ejemplo de error:*

- Prompt: "Escríbeme un informe."

- Resultado: Texto muy general, sin estructura clara ni enfoque definido.

*Mejor práctica:*

- Prompt mejorado: "Escríbeme un informe de 1000 palabras sobre los efectos del cambio climático en la agricultura en América Latina, con datos actuales, formato académico y lenguaje sencillo."

## 2. Usar la herramienta equivocada para el objetivo

Muchas personas usan la IA sin conocer qué tipo de modelo o herramienta es adecuada para cada tarea. Por ejemplo, usar una IA generadora de texto para hacer cálculos complejos en lugar de una hoja de cálculo con IA.

*Solución:* Conocer las principales herramientas disponibles (como vimos en el capítulo 4) y sus casos de uso.

## 3. No verificar los resultados

La IA puede inventar datos, mezclar hechos o generar información incorrecta. Este fenómeno es conocido como "alucinación de la IA". Por eso, siempre es necesario verificar la información generada, sobre todo si se trata de contenido técnico, científico o sensible.

## 4. Ignorar la privacidad y los datos sensibles

Muchas personas introducen información personal o confidencial en plataformas de IA sin saber cómo se manejan esos datos. Es fundamental revisar las políticas de privacidad y tener cuidado con lo que se comparte.

## 5. Depender completamente de la IA

La IA debe ser una herramienta de apoyo, no un reemplazo absoluto de la creatividad, el juicio crítico o el conocimiento humano. El mejor uso de la IA ocurre cuando se combina con la experiencia y criterio del usuario.

## Limitaciones técnicas de la IA

## 1. Conocimiento limitado al entrenamiento

La mayoría de las IA (especialmente los modelos de lenguaje) funcionan con información obtenida hasta cierta fecha de corte. Esto significa que no están actualizadas en tiempo real y pueden no tener acceso a datos recientes.

## 2. Falta de sentido común o comprensión profunda

Aunque los modelos pueden generar respuestas coherentes, no entienden el mundo como lo hace un ser humano. No tienen conciencia, emociones ni sentido común. Esto limita su capacidad para interpretar situaciones complejas o ambiguas.

## 3. Dependencia de grandes volúmenes de datos

Las IA más poderosas requieren grandes cantidades de datos para entrenarse, lo cual puede ser costoso y generar sesgos si los datos no son diversos o equilibrados.

## 4. Bias o sesgos incorporados

La IA puede replicar o incluso amplificar los sesgos presentes en los datos con los que fue entrenada. Esto puede llevar a resultados discriminatorios o injustos si no se controlan adecuadamente.

## 5. Problemas con idiomas minoritarios o no estándar

Muchos modelos de IA tienen un rendimiento inferior en idiomas con menor representación en los datos de entrenamiento, o con variantes locales muy específicas.

## Consejos para evitar errores y mitigar limitaciones

1. **Aprende a crear buenos prompts.** Cuanto más específico y claro seas, mejores resultados obtendrás.

2. **Verifica siempre la información.** Usa fuentes externas para confirmar datos importantes.

3. **Combina herramientas.** No todas las tareas deben resolverse con un solo tipo de IA.

4. **Educa a tu equipo.** Si trabajas con más personas, asegúrate de que todos entiendan cómo usar la IA correctamente.

5. **Sé consciente de los límites.** Usa la IA como complemento, no como sustituto total del criterio humano.

# 15

# El futuro de la IA: Tendencias y predicciones

La inteligencia artificial no es una moda pasajera; está en el corazón de la próxima gran transformación tecnológica. En este último capítulo vamos a analizar hacia dónde se dirige la IA, qué tendencias están marcando su evolución y cómo podemos prepararnos para aprovechar al máximo su potencial.

## 1. Modelos más potentes y especializados

Una tendencia clara es el desarrollo de modelos de IA más grandes y potentes, pero también más especializados. En lugar de una única IA general, veremos modelos diseñados para tareas muy concretas: redacción legal, diseño de videojuegos, diagnósticos médicos, gestión empresarial, etc.

- *Ejemplo real:* Bloomberg desarrolló un modelo propio de IA centrado en finanzas que entiende mejor la jerga del sector que modelos generales como GPT.

- *Qué esperar:* Las empresas y profesionales podrán usar IAs afinadas específicamente para sus necesidades, lo que aumentará la precisión y el valor de las soluciones.

## 2. Integración total en productos y servicios

La IA dejará de ser una herramienta independiente para convertirse en una parte invisible pero esencial de las aplicaciones cotidianas. Desde el correo electrónico que redacta respuestas automáticas hasta sistemas de gestión que predicen necesidades del cliente antes de que este lo sepa.

- *Ejemplo*: Gmail ya sugiere respuestas automáticas gracias al aprendizaje automático.

- *Futuro cercano:* Software de gestión de proyectos que detecte cuellos de botella, herramientas de ventas que identifiquen oportunidades sin intervención humana, etc.

## 3. IA generativa multimodal

Hasta ahora, las IA han sido buenas en tareas aisladas: texto, imagen o audio. La próxima generación combinará todo esto en un solo modelo capaz de recibir y generar contenido multimodal.

- *Qué significa:* Podrás pedir a una IA que lea un documento, lo resuma en audio, cree una presentación visual y redacte un email de seguimiento. Todo desde un solo prompt.

## 4. IA colaborativa en tiempo real

Pasamos de usar la IA como herramienta a trabajar con ella como si fuera un colega. En herramientas como Google Docs o Notion, ya están apareciendo asistentes en tiempo real que ayudan a escribir, corregir y enriquecer contenido.

- *Próximo paso:* Asistentes conversacionales que participen activamente en videollamadas, resuman discusiones y propongan acciones mientras el equipo trabaja.

## 5. Democratización del desarrollo de IA

Antes, desarrollar modelos de IA estaba limitado a grandes empresas con enormes presupuestos. Con nuevas plataformas de bajo código o sin código, cualquier persona podrá crear su propia IA personalizada.

- *Herramientas clave:* Microsoft Copilot Studio, Builder.ai, Peltarion, etc.

- **Impacto:** Emprendedores, educadores, pequeñas empresas y creadores podrán desarrollar soluciones de IA sin conocimientos técnicos profundos.

## 6. IA emocional y empática

Una línea de investigación que está ganando terreno es el desarrollo de IAs capaces de identificar y responder a emociones humanas. Aunque aún está en una etapa temprana, tiene mucho potencial en salud mental, atención al cliente y educación.

- *Ejemplo:* Woebot es un chatbot diseñado para ofrecer apoyo psicológico utilizando IA.

- *Riesgos:* Debates éticos sobre manipulación emocional, privacidad y confianza.

## 7. IA consciente del contexto y personalización total

Gracias a la combinación de datos históricos, comportamiento en tiempo real y sensores, la IA podrá adaptarse a cada persona de forma hiperpersonalizada.

- *Ejemplo futuro:* Un asistente que no solo recuerde tus tareas, sino que sepa cuándo hablar contigo, qué tono usar y cómo presentarte la información.

## 8. Regulación y gobernanza de la IA

Con su expansión global, los gobiernos están empezando a legislar sobre el uso ético, la privacidad y la responsabilidad de los sistemas de IA. Habrá un equilibrio necesario entre innovación y regulación.

- *Ejemplo actual:* La Unión Europea ha propuesto una Ley de Inteligencia Artificial que clasifica los usos según el nivel de riesgo.

## 9. Conciencia pública y alfabetización digital

Cada vez más personas entienden que la IA no es magia, sino una tecnología con posibilidades y riesgos. La formación en el uso responsable de la IA será parte de la educación básica, tanto en escuelas como en el mundo profesional.

- *Iniciativas clave:* Cursos de IA para no técnicos, programas en universidades, bootcamps accesibles, materiales en línea gratuitos.

## 10. IA en nuevos sectores: Agricultura, justicia, energía y más

Además de los sectores tradicionales, la IA comenzará a penetrar en áreas menos digitalizadas:

- Agricultura de precisión con drones e IA.

- Evaluación de pruebas legales con IA.

- Gestión energética predictiva basada en consumo y clima.

# Conclusión: El rol del usuario en el futuro de la IA

Más allá de los avances técnicos, el verdadero impacto de la IA lo marcarán los usuarios: cómo se entrena, cómo se usa, con qué objetivos y bajo qué valores. Como usuario principiante o intermedio, tienes el poder de usar la IA de forma creativa, responsable y estratégica.

Este libro ha sido una guía para ayudarte a empezar ese camino. La IA está en constante cambio, pero si entiendes sus fundamentos, sus posibilidades y sus riesgos, estarás mejor preparado para navegar su futuro.

La pregunta no es si la IA va a cambiar el mundo, sino qué papel vas a jugar tú en ese cambio

# Tabla de herramientas y usos de la IA

| Nombre de la IA | URL | Uso principal |
| --- | --- | --- |
| ChatGPT | https://chat.openai.com | Generación de texto, redacción, preguntas y respuestas |
| DALL·E | https://openai.com/dall-e | Generación de imágenes a partir de texto |
| MidJourney | https://www.midjourney.com | Creación de arte e ilustraciones desde prompts |
| Bard (ahora Gemini) | https://gemini.google.com | Chat conversacional, asistencia de Google |
| Claude | https://claude.ai | Asistente conversacional centrado en seguridad y ética |
| Copilot de GitHub | https://github.com/features/copilot | Asistencia a programadores, autocompletado de código |
| Notion AI | https://www.notion.so/product/ai | Redacción de documentos, resúmenes, brainstorming |
| Runway ML | https://runwayml.com | Generación de video y edición con IA |
| Pictory | https://pictory.ai | Crear videos a partir de artículos y texto |
| Canva (con IA) | https://www.canva.com | Diseño gráfico asistido con IA |
| Descript | https://www.descript.com | Edición de audio y video con transcripción automática |
| Tableau + IA | https://www.tableau.com | Visualización y análisis de datos con IA |
| Microsoft Azure ML | https://azure.microsoft.com/en-us/services/machine-learning/ | Plataforma de entrenamiento de modelos de IA |
| Google AutoML | https://cloud.google.com/automl | Herramientas de machine learning para no expertos |
| Zapier + AI | https://zapier.com | Automatización de tareas con ayuda de IA |
| ElevenLabs | https://www.elevenlabs.io | Generación de voz realista con IA |
| Leonardo AI | https://leonardo.ai | Generación de imágenes y contenido visual |

Esta tabla resume las herramientas más relevantes mencionadas a lo largo del libro, junto con su acceso directo y su uso principal. Puedes usarla como referencia rápida para explorar nuevas posibilidades